MASTERING FINANCIAL ACCOUNTING

A Comprehensive Guide for Business Students and Accountants

INCREASE YOUR ACADEMIC AND ACCOUNTING PERFORMANCE BY USING THIS COMPREHENSIVE GUIDE

DR. LESTER G REID

The Author of "Problem-Based Learning: The Handbook for Instructors and Scholars."

Copyright

The contents of this book, including but not limited to text, images, and illustrations, are protected under the copyright laws of United States of America and international conventions. The author and publisher have made every effort to ensure that the information provided in this book is accurate and up to date at the time of publication.

Unauthorized reproduction or distribution of any part of this book is prohibited. This includes but is not limited to copying, scanning, or distributing in any form or by any means, including electronic, mechanical, photocopying, recording, or otherwise, without the prior written permission of the author and publisher.

Copyright © 202 by Dr. Lester Reid

ISBN: 978 -17340601-3-3

Global Higher Education Institute Publishing

About This Book

Mastering Financial Accounting: A Comprehensive Guide for Business Students and Accountants is a valuable resource that aims to equip readers with a thorough understanding of the principles and practices of financial accounting. This comprehensive guide is designed to cater to both business students and professionals in the accounting field, providing them with the knowledge and skills necessary to excel in financial accounting.

The title itself, Mastering Financial Accounting: A Comprehensive Guide for Business Students and Accountants, conveys the intention of the guide to go beyond basic comprehension and enable readers to achieve mastery in this critical discipline. Financial accounting serves as the language of business, allowing organizations to communicate their financial performance and position to stakeholders. Mastering financial accounting is essential for making informed decisions, analyzing financial data, and ensuring compliance with accounting standards and regulations.

The guide covers a wide range of topics, starting with the fundamental principles and concepts of financial accounting. It provides a solid foundation by explaining the accounting equation, double-entry bookkeeping, and the basic elements of financial statements. The book then progresses to more advanced topics, including the recognition, measurement, and reporting of various assets, liabilities, equity, revenues, and expenses.

One of the strengths of this guide is its emphasis on practical application. It goes beyond theoretical explanations by providing real-world examples, case studies, and exercises that simulate actual accounting scenarios. This approach allows readers to develop the necessary skills to apply financial accounting concepts in practical situations. By mastering these skills, both students and accountants can confidently analyze financial statements, interpret financial data, and make informed decisions.

The guide also recognizes the importance of technology in modern financial accounting. It addresses the integration of accounting software and technology tools, highlighting how they can enhance efficiency, accuracy, and reporting capabilities. Readers will gain insights into the use of accounting software for recording transactions, generating financial reports, and automating routine accounting tasks.

Furthermore, the guide recognizes the evolving landscape of financial accounting and the impact of international financial reporting standards. It provides an overview of the key differences between various accounting frameworks, such as Generally Accepted Accounting Principles (GAAP) and International Financial Reporting Standards (IFRS). This knowledge is crucial for professionals working in multinational organizations or preparing financial statements for global audiences.

Another valuable aspect of this comprehensive guide is its focus on the role of financial accounting in decision-making and performance evaluation. It explores how financial statements are used to assess the financial health of an organization, evaluate profitability, analyze trends, and support strategic planning. By understanding the relationship between financial accounting and decision-making, readers can contribute to the overall success of their organizations.

Mastering Financial Accounting: A Comprehensive Guide for Business Students and Accountants is a must-have resource for anyone seeking to gain a deep understanding of financial accounting. It caters to both students embarking on their accounting journey and professionals looking to enhance their skills. With its comprehensive coverage, practical approach, and emphasis on real-world application, this guide equips readers with the knowledge and tools to excel in financial accounting and contribute to the financial success of their organizations.

Acknowledge

I would like to express my deepest gratitude to all those who have supported and contributed to the creation of this book, "Mastering Financial Accounting: A Comprehensive Guide for Business Students and Accountants." It is with great pleasure that I extend my sincerest appreciation to the following individuals:

To my loving family, thank you for your unwavering support, encouragement, and understanding throughout this journey. Your constant belief in me and my passion for accounting has been a driving force behind my dedication to this project. I am truly grateful for your love and encouragement.

To my students, both past and present, thank you for inspiring me to delve deeper into the world of financial accounting. Your curiosity and enthusiasm for learning have motivated me to create a comprehensive guide that caters to your needs and enhances your understanding of this complex discipline.

To my clients, who have entrusted me with their financial matters, thank you for your ongoing collaboration and the opportunity to apply the principles of financial accounting in real-world scenarios. Your feedback and challenges have deepened my understanding of the practical applications of this field.

To my colleagues, thank you for your support, collaboration, and intellectual discussions. Your insights and perspectives have been instrumental in refining the concepts and examples included in this book. The exchange of ideas and shared experiences have enriched my understanding of financial accounting.

To the publishers, editors, and the entire team involved in bringing this book to fruition, thank you for your professionalism, expertise, and dedication. Your commitment to excellence has ensured the highest quality of content and presentation, making this book a valuable resource for students and professionals alike.

Lastly, but certainly not least, I would like to express my gratitude to the readers of this book. It is my sincere hope that "Mastering Financial Accounting" serves as a valuable companion, guiding you through the intricacies of financial accounting and empowering you to excel in your academic pursuits or professional endeavors.

Without the support, guidance, and collaboration of all these individuals, this book would not have been possible. I am forever grateful for their contributions and the impact they have had on my journey as an educator and author.

Thank you all for being a part of this incredible endeavor.

Table of Contents

Preface

Welcome to "Mastering Financial Accounting: A Comprehensive Guide for Business Students and Accountants." This book has been specifically designed to provide you with a solid foundation in the principles and practices of financial accounting. Whether you are a business student aspiring to pursue a career in accounting or an accountant looking to deepen your knowledge and skills, this book is a valuable resource that will help you navigate the complexities of financial accounting with confidence.

Financial accounting is a fundamental aspect of business, providing vital information about an organization's financial health, performance, and overall stability. As businesses operate in an increasingly complex and dynamic environment, the demand for skilled financial accountants continues to grow. This book aims to equip you with the necessary knowledge and tools to excel in this field.

Key Features of the Book:

1. **Comprehensive Coverage:** The book covers all the essential topics of financial accounting, from the basics to more advanced concepts. Starting with an introduction to financial accounting, we examine topics such as the accounting cycle, financial statements and reporting, revenue recognition, expense measurement, assets and liabilities, equity, financial analysis, and more. Each chapter is carefully structured to provide a thorough understanding of the topic, supported by clear explanations, examples, and practice exercises.

2. **Practical Approach:** We believe in bridging the gap between theory and practice. Throughout the book, we provide real-world examples and case studies to illustrate how financial accounting concepts are applied in actual business scenarios. By connecting theory to practice, you will gain valuable insights into how financial accounting principles are utilized to make informed business decisions.

3. **Clarity and Accessibility:** Financial accounting can be a complex subject, but we strive to present the material in a clear and accessible manner. We use concise language, avoid jargon whenever possible, and provide step-by-step explanations of key concepts and processes. Complex topics are broken down into manageable sections, ensuring that you can grasp the material at your own pace.

4. **Interactive Learning Tools:** To enhance your learning experience, the book includes various interactive elements. These include practice exercises, review questions, and case studies that allow you to apply the concepts you have learned. Additionally, we provide online resources such as quizzes, solutions manuals, and supplementary materials to further support your understanding and reinforce your knowledge.

5. **Practical Tips and Insights:** Throughout the book, we provide practical tips and insights gleaned from our experience as accountants and educators. These insights offer valuable guidance on best practices,

common challenges, and emerging trends in financial accounting. By incorporating these tips into your learning journey, you will develop a well-rounded perspective on the profession and its practical applications.

This book is suitable for both self-study and classroom use. Whether you are studying independently or as part of a structured course, each chapter is designed to facilitate your learning experience. You can use the book as a comprehensive guide, following the sequential order of the chapters, or you can focus on specific topics of interest.

I believe that financial accounting is not just a subject to be learned but a skill to be mastered. With dedication and practice, you can develop proficiency in financial accounting and unlock a world of opportunities in the business and accounting fields. "Mastering Financial Accounting: A Comprehensive Guide for Business Students and Accountants" is here to accompany you on this journey, providing you with the knowledge, skills, and confidence to excel in financial accounting.

I hope that you find this book valuable and that it serves as a trusted companion in your exploration of financial accounting. I encourage you to engage actively with the material, ask questions, seek clarification, and apply the concepts to real-world situations. By doing so, you will build a strong foundation in financial accounting and set yourself up for success in your academic and professional endeavors.

Best wishes on your journey to mastering financial accounting!

CHAPTER ONE
About the Field of Accounting

The field of accounting encompasses various classifications, each serving a unique purpose in the financial management of a business. These classifications are essential for organizing and analyzing financial information, enabling businesses to make informed decisions and comply with regulatory requirements. Here, we will discuss the areas of accounting and their significance to businesses:

1. **Financial Accounting:** Financial accounting focuses on the preparation and reporting of financial statements for external users, such as investors, creditors, and regulatory authorities. It involves the recording, summarizing, and communication of financial transactions in accordance with Generally Accepted Accounting Principles (GAAP) or International Financial Reporting Standards (IFRS). The financial statements, including the balance sheet, income statement, statement of cash flows, and statement of changes in equity, provide a comprehensive overview of a company's financial position and performance. Financial accounting ensures transparency, enables stakeholders to evaluate a company's financial health, and facilitates decision-making.

2. **Managerial Accounting:** Managerial accounting, also known as cost accounting, is concerned with providing information for internal users, primarily management, to support planning, control, and

decision-making processes. It involves analyzing and interpreting financial data to aid in strategic planning, budgeting, cost analysis, and performance evaluation. Managerial accounting focuses on producing detailed reports, such as budgets, variance analysis, and profitability analysis, to help managers make informed decisions and optimize resource allocation. It plays a critical role in operational efficiency, cost control, and improving overall business performance.

3. **Tax Accounting:** Tax accounting involves the preparation and filing of tax returns in compliance with tax laws and regulations. It focuses on accurately calculating and reporting income, deductions, and credits to determine a business's tax liability. Tax accountants stay updated with tax laws and regulations, identify tax-saving opportunities, and ensure compliance to avoid penalties and maximize tax benefits. They assist businesses in managing their tax obligations effectively and strategize tax planning to minimize tax liabilities within legal boundaries.

4. **Auditing:** Auditing is the examination and evaluation of financial records, systems, and processes to ensure accuracy, integrity, and compliance. External auditors, often independent professionals, conduct audits to provide an objective assessment of a company's financial statements and internal controls. Internal auditors, on the other hand, work within the organization to assess risk management, internal control effectiveness, and

operational efficiency. Auditing provides assurance to stakeholders regarding the reliability of financial information, detects errors or fraud, and enhances transparency and trust in financial reporting.

5. **Governmental and Nonprofit Accounting:** Governmental and nonprofit accounting focuses on accounting principles and practices specific to government agencies and nonprofit organizations. These entities have unique reporting requirements and are subject to specialized accounting standards, such as the Governmental Accounting Standards Board (GASB) for government entities and the Financial Accounting Standards Board (FASB) for nonprofits. This classification ensures proper financial reporting and accountability in the public sector and nonprofit sector, where transparency, accountability, and compliance with specific regulations are paramount.

The areas of accounting - financial accounting, managerial accounting, tax accounting, auditing, and governmental and nonprofit accounting - each serve a vital purpose in the financial management of a business. They provide essential information for decision-making, regulatory compliance, financial reporting, and performance evaluation. By understanding and effectively utilizing these classifications, businesses can maintain accurate financial records, make informed decisions, ensure compliance, and drive overall success.

The field of accounting plays a critical role in the functioning of businesses, organizations, and economies worldwide. It encompasses a wide range of activities related to the recording, analysis, interpretation, and reporting of financial information. Accounting provides a structured framework for businesses to track their financial transactions, make informed decisions, and communicate their financial health to stakeholders.

Accountants are responsible for various tasks, including bookkeeping, financial analysis, budgeting, auditing, tax planning, and financial reporting. They ensure that financial records are accurate, comply with legal and regulatory requirements, and provide valuable insights for management and external stakeholders. Accounting serves as the language of business, enabling effective communication between different stakeholders, such as investors, creditors, managers, and government entities. It helps in evaluating the financial performance and position of a company, assessing its profitability, liquidity, and solvency.

The field of accounting offers numerous career opportunities, including roles such as auditors, tax consultants, financial analysts, management accountants, and controllers. Accountants work in various sectors, including public accounting firms, corporations, government agencies, nonprofit organizations, and consulting firms. Advancements in technology have significantly impacted the field of accounting, with the introduction of sophisticated accounting software, automation, and data analytics. Accountants now have access to advanced tools that streamline processes, improve accuracy, and provide real-time financial insights.

Ethics and integrity are fundamental principles in the field of accounting. Accountants are expected to adhere to professional standards, maintain confidentiality, and exercise objectivity and impartiality in their work. They play a crucial role in promoting transparency, accountability, and trust in financial transactions. The field of accounting is essential for the smooth operation of businesses and the proper allocation of resources. It provides valuable financial information that enables decision-making, supports strategic planning, and ensures compliance with legal and regulatory requirements. With its wide range of career opportunities and its impact on the business world, accounting continues to be a dynamic and influential field.

Financial Accounting Career Opportunities

Financial accounting offers a wide range of career opportunities for accounting students. These careers provide diverse roles in various industries and organizations, offering the chance to work with financial data, analyze financial statements, ensure regulatory compliance, and provide financial insights. Let's explore some of the financial accounting careers that accounting students can pursue:

1. **Public Accountant:** Public accountants work for accounting firms, providing auditing, tax, and consulting services to clients. They perform financial statement audits, examine financial records, ensure compliance with accounting standards, and provide guidance on financial reporting. Public accountants often pursue Certified Public Accountant (CPA) certification to enhance their career prospects.

2. **Financial Analyst:** Financial analysts analyze financial data, prepare financial reports, and provide insights to support investment decisions. They assess financial performance, analyze industry trends, conduct risk assessments, and evaluate investment opportunities. Financial analysts work in various settings, including banks, investment firms, corporations, and government agencies.

3. **Internal Auditor:** Internal auditors evaluate an organization's internal controls, risk management processes, and compliance with regulations. They review financial records, identify control weaknesses, and recommend improvements to enhance operational efficiency and mitigate risks. Internal auditors play a critical role in ensuring that organizations operate ethically and efficiently.

4. **Financial Controller:** Financial controllers oversee financial operations within an organization. They manage accounting processes, prepare financial statements, develop budgets, and ensure compliance with accounting standards and regulations. Financial controllers also provide financial analysis, strategic guidance, and support decision-making by senior management.

5. **Tax Accountant:** Tax accountants specialize in tax planning and compliance. They prepare tax returns, analyze tax implications of business transactions, and ensure compliance with tax laws and regulations. Tax accountants stay up-to-date with tax laws and

provide guidance on minimizing tax liabilities while maximizing tax benefits.

6. **Cost Accountant:** Cost accountants focus on analyzing and controlling costs within an organization. They track and analyze expenses, calculate product costs, and provide insights to improve cost-efficiency. Cost accountants play a vital role in budgeting, pricing decisions, and cost control strategies.

7. **Financial Manager:** Financial managers oversee the financial operations of an organization, including financial planning, budgeting, and reporting. They analyze financial data, develop strategies to improve profitability, manage cash flow, and make investment decisions. Financial managers collaborate with various departments to ensure financial objectives are met.

8. **Risk Manager:** Risk managers assess and manage financial risks within organizations. They identify potential risks, develop risk management strategies, and implement controls to mitigate risks. Risk managers analyze financial data, conduct risk assessments, and ensure compliance with regulatory requirements.

These are just a few examples of the diverse career opportunities available in financial accounting. The field offers stability, growth potential, and the opportunity to work with a wide range of clients and industries. With the right education, certifications, and experience, individuals can build successful and rewarding careers in financial accounting. In addition to these roles, accounting students can explore careers as financial consultants, forensic accountants, investment bankers, financial systems analysts, or financial educators. Graduates can also consider working in government agencies, non-profit organizations, or starting their own accounting practices.

To pursue these careers, accounting students should consider acquiring relevant certifications such as the CPA, Certified Management Accountant (CMA), or Certified Internal Auditor (CIA) depending on their career goals. Gaining practical experience through internships or entry-level positions is also valuable in building a successful financial accounting career.

Financial accounting offers a range of rewarding career paths for accounting students. The field provides opportunities to work with financial data, contribute to decision-making processes, and play a critical role in the financial success of organizations across various industries. Financial accounting offers a wide range of career opportunities for individuals who have an interest in working with numbers, analyzing financial data, and providing valuable insights to businesses and organizations.

The demand for skilled financial accountants continues to grow across industries, making it an attractive career choice for individuals with a passion for numbers, attention to detail, and analytical skills. The diverse range of career paths ensures that individuals can find opportunities that align with their interests and expertise.

To excel in the field of financial accounting, it is essential to obtain relevant education and certifications, such as a Bachelor's or Master's degree in accounting, and pursue professional certifications such as Certified Public Accountant (CPA), Certified Management Accountant (CMA), or Chartered Financial Analyst (CFA), depending on the chosen career path.

Furthermore, continuous learning and staying up-to-date with changing regulations, technological advancements, and industry trends are crucial for professional growth and advancement in financial accounting careers. Building strong analytical, communication, and problem-solving skills will also contribute to success in this field.

Financial accounting offers a rewarding and challenging career that combines technical expertise, business acumen, and the opportunity to contribute to the financial success and stability of organizations. With the potential for growth, diverse career paths, and the importance of financial information in decision-making, pursuing a career in financial accounting can lead to a fulfilling and prosperous professional journey.

Before Choosing a Career in Accounting

Choosing a career is a significant decision that requires careful thought and consideration. When it comes to accounting, there are several key factors to explore before making a final choice. Accounting offers a wide range of opportunities and can be a rewarding career path for individuals with the right skills and interests. Here are some important considerations to keep in mind before embarking on a career in accounting.

First and foremost, it is crucial to assess your aptitude for numbers and analytical thinking. Accounting is a field that requires strong mathematical skills, attention to detail, and the ability to analyze and interpret financial information. If you enjoy working with numbers, solving complex problems, and have a meticulous nature, accounting may be a suitable career option for you.

Before choosing a career in accounting, accounting major students should consider the following steps to ensure they make an informed decision:

1. **Self-Assessment:** Accounting students should conduct a self-assessment to determine their interests, skills, and strengths. Consider what aspects of accounting you enjoy, whether it's financial analysis, auditing, tax, or management accounting. Assess your quantitative skills, attention to detail, problem-solving abilities, and communication skills, as these are crucial in the accounting profession.

2. **Research:** Explore the various career paths within the accounting field. Research the different roles and responsibilities associated with each career option. Understand the educational requirements, certifications, and skills needed for each path. Consider the industry sectors that interest you, such as public accounting, corporate accounting, government accounting, or nonprofit accounting.

3. **Network and Informational Interviews:** Connect with professionals in the accounting field through networking events, career fairs, and informational interviews. Reach out to alumni, professors, and professionals working in different accounting roles to gain insights into their experiences and the realities of the profession. This will help you understand the day-to-day work, challenges, and opportunities in different accounting careers.

4. **Internships and Work Experience:** Seek internships or part-time positions in accounting firms, corporations, or other organizations to gain practical experience. Internships provide hands-on exposure to accounting tasks, allowing you to assess whether the work aligns with your interests and goals. Practical experience also enhances your resume and increases your chances of securing a job after graduation.

5. **Professional Certifications:** Research professional certifications relevant to the accounting field, such as the Certified Public Accountant (CPA), Certified Management Accountant (CMA), Certified Internal Auditor (CIA), or Chartered Financial Analyst (CFA). Understand the requirements, eligibility criteria, and career benefits associated with each certification. Obtaining certifications can provide a competitive advantage and open up more career opportunities.

6. **Seek Guidance from Faculty and Career Services:** Consult with accounting faculty members and career services advisors at your educational institution. They can provide guidance, resources, and information on career options, job market trends, and potential pathways in the accounting field. They may also assist with resume building, interview preparation, and connecting you with alumni or industry professionals.

7. **Attend Accounting Events and Conferences:** Participate in accounting events, conferences, and workshops to stay updated on industry trends, regulatory changes, and emerging technologies in the accounting profession. These events offer opportunities to network, learn from industry experts, and gain insights into the evolving landscape of accounting.

8. **Consider Long-Term Goals:** Reflect on your long-term career goals and aspirations. Consider factors such as work-life balance, career progression opportunities, potential for specialization, and the potential for growth in your chosen accounting career. Determine if the accounting field aligns with your personal and professional goals.

By taking these steps before choosing a career in accounting, accounting major students can gain a better understanding of the profession, explore various options, and make an informed decision that aligns with their interests, skills, and long-term aspirations. Remember that career choices are personal, and it's essential to choose a path that resonates with your goals, values, and aspirations.

Another important aspect to consider is the educational requirements. Most accounting positions require at least a bachelor's degree in accounting or a related field. Research reputable educational institutions and programs that offer comprehensive accounting curricula. It is also advisable to look into professional certifications such as Certified Public Accountant (CPA) or Chartered Accountant (CA), as these designations can enhance your career prospects and provide a competitive edge in the job market.

Internships and practical experience play a vital role in gaining a deeper understanding of the accounting profession. Seek out internships or entry-level positions that offer hands-on experience in accounting practices. This allows you to apply theoretical knowledge to real-world scenarios and gain insights into the day-to-day tasks and responsibilities of an accountant. Additionally, internships provide an opportunity to network with professionals in the field, which can be invaluable for future career prospects.

Consider the different areas of accounting and their specific job roles. Financial accounting, management accounting, tax accounting, and auditing are some common specializations within the field. Research each area to understand the specific skills and responsibilities required. This will help you determine which branch of accounting aligns best with your interests, strengths, and long-term career goals.

When contemplating a career in accounting, it is essential to evaluate the potential for growth and advancement. Accounting offers a clear career progression path, with opportunities to move up to management positions or specialize in specific industries. Consider the long-term prospects and the demand for accountants in different sectors. Assess the growth potential and determine if it aligns with your professional aspirations.

Work-life balance is another factor to consider. Some accounting roles, such as tax or auditing, may have busy periods that require long hours. Consider your personal preferences and how they align with the demands of different accounting positions. Assess your ability to manage workloads, deadlines, and potential stress associated with specific roles.

Networking and professional development are essential aspects of a successful accounting career. Building a professional network through industry events, joining accounting associations, and connecting with professionals can open doors to opportunities, mentorship, and career advice. Additionally, continuous learning and staying updated on accounting regulations, industry trends, and technological advancements are crucial to stay competitive in the field. Seek guidance and advice from professionals in the accounting industry, career counselors, or academic advisors. They can provide insights into the field, share their experiences, and offer guidance based on your unique circumstances and aspirations.

While accounting can be a financially rewarding career, it is essential to consider the financial aspects associated with pursuing this path. Assess the cost of education, potential student loans, and the return on investment of your accounting degree. Research the average salary ranges for entry-level accountants and the potential for salary growth as you progress in your career.

Before choosing a career in accounting, it is important to assess your skills, educational requirements, and personal interests. Gain practical experience through internships, explore different specializations within the field, evaluate long-term growth prospects, and consider work-life balance. Networking, continuous professional development, and seeking guidance are key steps to ensure a successful and fulfilling career in accounting. By taking the time to explore these factors, you can make an informed decision and set yourself up for a rewarding career in the field of accounting.

Finally, take the time for personal reflection and self-assessment. Consider your personal values, interests, and strengths. Evaluate how accounting aligns with your skills and long-term aspirations. Assess whether you enjoy problem-solving, attention to detail, and working with financial information. Reflecting on your personal goals and passions will help you determine if a career in accounting is the right fit for you. By thoroughly evaluating these factors, you can make an informed decision about pursuing a fulfilling and successful career in accounting. Remember to seek advice from professionals, career counselors, and mentors who can provide valuable insights and guidance along the way.

Financial Accounting Careers Salaries

When considering a career in financial accounting, one important aspect that often comes to mind is salary. Financial accounting careers offer a range of opportunities with varying salary levels based on factors such as experience, qualifications, industry, location, and job responsibilities.

The salaries for financial accounting careers can vary significantly depending on factors such as education, experience, industry, location, and the size of the organization. However, I can provide you with a general idea of the salary ranges for some common financial accounting careers:

1. **Public Accountant:** Entry-level positions in public accounting firms typically offer salaries ranging from $50,000 to $70,000 per year. As accountants gain experience and advance to managerial or senior positions, salaries can range from $70,000 to $150,000 or more annually. Partners or owners in accounting firms can earn significantly higher incomes.

2. **Financial Analyst:** Entry-level financial analyst positions often start in the range of $50,000 to $70,000 per year. With experience and expertise, financial analysts can progress to senior or managerial roles, where salaries can range from $70,000 to $150,000 or more annually, depending on the industry and location.

3. **Internal Auditor:** Internal auditors typically earn salaries starting from $55,000 to $75,000 per year at the entry level. As they gain experience and move into senior or managerial roles, salaries can range from $75,000 to $120,000 or more annually

4. **Financial Controller:** Financial controllers generally earn salaries ranging from $80,000 to $150,000 or more per year, depending on the size and complexity of the organization, industry, and geographic location.

5. **Tax Accountant:** Entry-level tax accountants can expect salaries in the range of $50,000 to $70,000 per year. With experience and specialized knowledge, tax accountants can progress to senior or managerial positions, where salaries can range from $70,000 to $120,000 or more annually.

6. **Cost Accountant:** Cost accountants typically earn salaries starting from $60,000 to $80,000 per year at the entry level. As they gain experience and move into senior roles, salaries can range from $80,000 to $120,000 or more annually.

7. **Financial Manager:** Financial managers' salaries can vary widely depending on the size and industry of the organization. Entry-level financial managers can earn salaries ranging from $70,000 to $100,000 per year, while experienced financial managers can earn salaries exceeding $150,000 or more annually.

8. **Risk Manager:** The salary range for risk managers can vary depending on the organization and industry. Entry-level positions may start around $60,000 to $80,000 per year, while experienced risk managers can earn salaries ranging from $80,000 to $150,000 or more annually.

It's important to note that these salary ranges are approximate and can vary significantly based on individual factors. Additionally, salaries can be higher in major financial centers and metropolitan areas compared to smaller towns or regions with a lower cost of living. Furthermore, obtaining relevant certifications such as the CPA, CMA, or CIA can positively impact salary potential in many financial accounting careers. It's advisable to research industry-specific salary data, consult salary surveys, and consider local market conditions to gain a more accurate understanding of the salary ranges for specific financial accounting careers.

It's essential to note that the salary ranges provided are approximate and can vary depending on factors such as geographic location, economic conditions, and the company's financial health. Additionally, career growth and salary potential in financial accounting can be influenced by continuous learning, professional certifications, and specialization in specific areas of expertise.

Financial accounting careers offer a wide range of salary levels based on various factors. From entry-level positions to senior executive roles, financial accountants can earn competitive salaries and enjoy opportunities for career advancement. It's important for individuals considering a career in financial accounting to research the industry, understand the required qualifications, and evaluate their long-term career goals to make informed decisions about their chosen path. By aligning their skills, interests, and aspirations with the salary potential of different financial accounting careers, individuals can set themselves up for a rewarding and financially fulfilling professional journey.

The field of financial accounting offers a wide range of career opportunities with varying salary levels. Salaries in financial accounting are influenced by several factors, including experience, qualifications, industry, location, and job responsibilities. Understanding the salary potential of different financial accounting careers can help individuals make informed decisions about their career paths.

Highest Paying States – Accounting Careers

When considering a career in accounting, one important aspect to consider is the potential earning potential in different locations. Salaries for accounting professionals can vary significantly depending on the state in which they work. Certain states offer higher compensation due to factors such as cost of living, demand for accounting services, and industry concentration.

The salaries in financial accounting careers can vary based on several factors, including location. While it's challenging to provide an exhaustive list of states with the highest salaries, the following states are generally known for offering higher compensation in the field of financial accounting:

1. **New York:** New York, particularly in major cities like New York City, offers some of the highest salaries for financial accounting professionals. The presence of numerous multinational corporations, financial institutions, and accounting firms contributes to the higher pay scales.

2. **California:** California is home to many technology companies, entertainment industry giants, and a thriving business environment. Cities such as San Francisco, Los Angeles, and San Diego offer competitive salaries for financial accounting professionals.

3. **Connecticut:** Connecticut is known for its strong finance and insurance sectors. Cities like Stamford and Hartford have a significant concentration of financial institutions and offer attractive salary packages for financial accounting roles.

4. **Massachusetts:** Massachusetts, and specifically the Greater Boston area, is renowned for its strong financial services industry and academic institutions. The presence of major corporations, investment firms, and consulting firms in the region contributes to higher salaries.

5. **New Jersey:** New Jersey has a diverse economy with a significant presence of pharmaceutical, healthcare, and financial services companies. Cities like Newark and Jersey City offer competitive salaries for financial accounting professionals.

6. **Texas:** Texas, with cities such as Houston and Dallas, is home to a robust energy sector, along with a diverse range of industries. The state offers competitive salaries for financial accounting professionals, particularly in the oil and gas industry.

7. **Illinois:** Illinois, and specifically Chicago, has a thriving business environment and a concentration of Fortune 500 companies. Financial accounting professionals in Chicago can expect competitive salaries due to the presence of major corporations and financial institutions.

8. **District of Columbia:** The District of Columbia, which includes Washington, D.C., offers higher salaries for financial accounting professionals due to the presence of government agencies, consulting firms, and nonprofit organizations.

It's important to note that salary levels can also be influenced by factors such as job experience, education, certifications, and the specific employer or industry. Additionally, the cost of living in each state should also be considered when evaluating salary potential. While these states are known for offering higher salaries, there may be opportunities for well-compensated financial accounting careers in other regions as well. It's advisable to research and consider multiple factors when assessing salary prospects in different states.

It is important to note that while these states tend to offer higher salaries for accounting professionals, the cost of living and other factors should also be taken into account. Additionally, salaries can vary within each state based on factors such as experience, education, certifications, and job responsibilities. Furthermore, demand for accounting professionals in specific industries or sectors can also influence salary levels. The highest paying states for accounting careers offer attractive compensation packages due to factors such as robust economies, industry concentrations, and competitive job markets.

The "Big 4" Accounting Companies in the World

The Big 4 firms, also known as the Big Four or the Four Horsemen, refer to the four largest multinational professional services firms in the world. These firms dominate the accounting industry and provide a wide range of services, including audit, tax, consulting, and advisory services to clients across various industries. The Big 4 firms are Deloitte, PricewaterhouseCoopers (PwC), Ernst & Young (EY), and KPMG.

1. **Deloitte:** Deloitte is one of the largest professional services firms globally, with a strong presence in audit, tax, consulting, and advisory services. It operates in more than 150 countries and serves clients ranging from small businesses to multinational corporations. Deloitte is known for its commitment to innovation, industry expertise, and providing holistic solutions to its clients' complex challenges.

2. **PricewaterhouseCoopers (PwC):** PwC is a global network of firms providing assurance, tax, and advisory services. With a presence in over 155 countries, PwC serves clients in diverse industries such as technology, finance, healthcare, and manufacturing. PwC is renowned for its focus on building trust and delivering quality services to its clients, helping them navigate the complexities of the business environment.

3. **Ernst & Young (EY):** EY is a multinational professional services firm with a strong global footprint. It offers services in assurance, tax, consulting, and advisory to clients across sectors. EY is known for its commitment to sustainable growth, digital transformation, and helping clients navigate regulatory challenges. The firm's global network allows it to bring together diverse perspectives and provide innovative solutions to clients' business needs.

4. **KPMG:** KPMG is a leading provider of audit, tax, and advisory services, operating in more than 150 countries. The firm serves clients across industries, including financial services, healthcare, technology, and manufacturing. KPMG is recognized for its expertise in risk management, governance, and helping clients address complex business issues. The firm is committed to delivering value and building long-term relationships with its clients.

These Big 4 firms are highly respected in the industry for several reasons:

1. **Global Presence:** The Big 4 firms have extensive global networks, allowing them to serve clients in multiple countries and provide cross-border services. This global reach enables them to handle complex multinational engagements and tap into a vast pool of resources and expertise.

2. **Industry Expertise:** The firms have specialized teams that possess deep knowledge and experience

in various industries. This industry-specific expertise enables them to understand clients' unique challenges and provide tailored solutions that address industry-specific regulations, trends, and issues.

3. **Professional Development:** The Big 4 firms offer extensive training and development programs to their professionals. Employees have access to ongoing learning opportunities, certifications, and mentorship, which helps them enhance their skills and knowledge in the accounting profession.

4. **Professional Standards:** The Big 4 firms adhere to strict professional standards and regulatory requirements. They are committed to maintaining high levels of integrity, ethics, and quality in their services. The firms invest significant resources in quality control systems and processes to ensure that their work meets the highest standards.

5. **Networking and Collaboration:** Working for a Big 4 firm provides access to a vast network of professionals and clients. This network allows employees to collaborate with experts from various fields, exchange ideas, and develop valuable relationships. The exposure to diverse clients and projects also contributes to professional growth and development.

6. **Career Opportunities:** The Big 4 firms offer a wide range of career opportunities and paths for professionals. Employees can specialize in areas

such as audit, tax, advisory, or consulting, and have opportunities to work with clients across industries and geographies. The firms also provide avenues for advancement and leadership roles within the organization.

While working at a Big 4 firm offers numerous advantages, it also comes with certain challenges. The demanding work environment, long hours, and high client expectations can create a demanding lifestyle. However, many professionals view these challenges as opportunities for personal and professional growth.

The Big 4 firms are global leaders in the accounting industry, providing a wide range of services to clients around the world. Their extensive networks, industry expertise, commitment to professional standards, and career opportunities make them highly sought after by accounting professionals. Working for a Big 4 firm offers a unique platform for learning, growth, and exposure to diverse clients and projects.

Pursuing a career at one of these firms offers several advantages:

1. **Global Presence and Reputation:** The Big 4 firms have a vast global network, with offices in multiple countries. They handle audits for some of the world's largest and most influential companies. Working at a Big 4 firm provides exposure to a wide range of clients, industries, and complex financial transactions. The firms' global reputation adds value

to your resume and opens doors for international opportunities.

2. **Learning and Development:** Big 4 firms invest heavily in training and professional development programs. They offer comprehensive training to enhance technical skills, industry knowledge, and soft skills such as communication and leadership. The firms provide opportunities for continuous learning, ensuring that employees stay up-to-date with accounting standards, regulations, and emerging trends.

3. **Variety of Work:** Working at a Big 4 firm offers exposure to diverse clients and projects. Auditors get the opportunity to work on different industries, ranging from financial services and technology to healthcare and manufacturing. This variety of work provides a broader understanding of business operations and financial practices across various sectors.

4. **Career Advancement:** The Big 4 firms provide clear career progression paths. Employees can start as entry-level associates and progress to senior roles, managers, and eventually partners. Advancement is based on performance, demonstrated skills, and commitment. The firms offer opportunities for specialization, allowing individuals to become subject matter experts in specific industries or areas of auditing.

5. **Networking Opportunities:** Working at a Big 4 firm exposes you to a vast professional network. You will collaborate with colleagues from diverse backgrounds, interact with clients and industry professionals, and attend networking events. These connections can be valuable throughout your career, providing opportunities for mentorship, referrals, and future job prospects.

6. **Exposure to Cutting-Edge Technology:** Big 4 firms are at the forefront of adopting and implementing technology in their audit processes. As an employee, you will have access to advanced audit tools and software that streamline and enhance auditing procedures. This exposure to technology-driven solutions will enhance your skill set and knowledge of industry best practices.

7. **Transferable Skills:** Working at a Big 4 firm equips you with transferable skills that are highly valued in the business world. These include analytical thinking, problem-solving, attention to detail, teamwork, and effective communication. These skills are not only applicable to auditing but can also be leveraged in other areas of finance, consulting, or management.

8. **Prestige and Career Opportunities:** Having Big 4 experience on your resume carries significant weight and is highly regarded by employers. The reputation and brand recognition of the Big 4 firms open doors to a wide range of career opportunities, both within and outside the accounting profession. Many

individuals who start their careers at a Big 4 firm go on to successful careers in finance, executive management, or entrepreneurship.

It's important to note that while pursuing a career at a Big 4 firm offers numerous benefits, it also requires dedication, long working hours, and a commitment to excellence. The work can be demanding, particularly during the peak audit season. However, the skills, experiences, and opportunities gained at a Big 4 firm can be instrumental in building a successful and rewarding career in the auditing profession.

A. Studying Financial Accounting

Studying financial accounting offers numerous benefits and opportunities for individuals interested in pursuing a career in business, finance, or related fields. Here are several compelling reasons why studying financial accounting is important:

1. **Foundation of Business Knowledge:** Financial accounting serves as the foundation of business knowledge. It provides a systematic understanding of how financial transactions are recorded, summarized, and communicated. By studying financial accounting, individuals develop a solid understanding of core financial concepts and principles that are essential for making informed business decisions.

2. **Business Decision-Making:** Financial accounting equips individuals with the skills to analyze financial

information and make effective business decisions. It helps in evaluating the financial performance and position of a company, assessing profitability, liquidity, and solvency, and identifying areas of strength or weakness. Understanding financial statements and ratios enables individuals to assess the financial health of an organization and make informed decisions about investments, lending, or business operations.

3. **Career Opportunities:** Financial accounting knowledge opens up a wide range of career opportunities. Accountants are in demand across industries, including public accounting firms, corporations, government agencies, and non-profit organizations. Studying financial accounting can lead to careers as auditors, financial analysts, controllers, tax professionals, or even entrepreneurship. It provides a versatile skill set that is valuable in various job roles and industries.

4. **Communication and Collaboration:** Financial accounting involves interpreting complex financial information and effectively communicating it to various stakeholders. Studying financial accounting enhances communication skills, enabling individuals to translate financial data into meaningful insights for non-financial professionals. This ability to collaborate and communicate with colleagues, clients, investors, and regulators is crucial in business environments where financial information needs to be shared and understood by diverse audiences.

5. **Compliance and Governance:** Financial accounting plays a critical role in compliance and governance. By studying financial accounting, individuals gain knowledge about relevant accounting standards, regulations, and ethical considerations. This understanding is essential for ensuring accurate financial reporting, maintaining transparency, and adhering to legal and regulatory requirements. In an era of increased scrutiny and accountability, professionals with financial accounting expertise are in high demand to ensure compliance with financial regulations and to maintain ethical business practices.

6. **Entrepreneurial Skills:** Studying financial accounting can be beneficial for aspiring entrepreneurs. It provides insights into financial planning, budgeting, and cash flow management, which are essential for running a successful business. Understanding financial statements helps entrepreneurs assess the financial viability of their ventures, attract investors, and make informed decisions to grow and sustain their businesses.

7. **Personal Financial Management:** Financial accounting knowledge is not only useful in the business context but also in personal financial management. Individuals can apply the principles of financial accounting to manage personal finances, budget effectively, understand investment options, and make informed decisions about saving, investing, and borrowing.

Studying financial accounting offers a strong foundation in business knowledge, enhances decision-making abilities, and opens up diverse career opportunities. It equips individuals with the skills to analyze financial data, communicate effectively, ensure compliance, and make informed business decisions. Whether pursuing a career in accounting or any other field, financial accounting knowledge is valuable for personal and professional growth. It provides individuals with a competitive edge and the ability to navigate the financial complexities of the business world.

B. Studying Managerial Accounting

Studying managerial accounting offers numerous advantages and opportunities for individuals interested in pursuing careers in business, management, or related fields. Managerial accounting provides crucial information and tools for effective decision-making within organizations. Here are several compelling reasons why studying managerial accounting is important:

1. **Internal Decision-Making:** Managerial accounting focuses on providing information for internal decision-making within organizations. It helps managers and executives analyze financial data and make informed decisions related to resource allocation, cost control, pricing strategies, product profitability, and budgeting. By studying managerial accounting, individuals gain the skills necessary to analyze and interpret financial information to support strategic and operational decision-making.

2. **Cost Analysis and Control:** Managerial accounting emphasizes the analysis and control of costs within organizations. Studying managerial accounting equips individuals with techniques such as cost-volume-profit analysis, budgeting, variance analysis, and activity-based costing. These tools help managers understand the cost structure of products or services, identify cost-saving opportunities, and improve operational efficiency.

3. **Performance Evaluation:** Managerial accounting provides frameworks and metrics to evaluate the performance of various business segments, departments, or projects within an organization. It enables managers to assess the profitability, efficiency, and effectiveness of different areas and make data-driven decisions to improve performance. Understanding managerial accounting enables individuals to measure and evaluate the success of strategies, initiatives, or investments.

4. **Planning and Forecasting:** Managerial accounting assists in the planning and forecasting processes within organizations. It provides techniques and tools to develop budgets, create financial projections, and set targets for future periods. By studying managerial accounting, individuals learn how to create realistic plans, set achievable goals, and monitor actual performance against projections.

5. **Strategic Decision-Making:** Managerial accounting plays a critical role in strategic decision-making. It helps managers assess the financial impact of potential investments, expansion plans, mergers, or acquisitions. By studying managerial accounting, individuals gain insights into assessing the financial feasibility and potential risks associated with strategic initiatives. They can evaluate the financial implications of alternative courses of action and make informed decisions that align with the organization's long-term goals.

6. **Communication and Collaboration:** Managerial accounting involves analyzing financial information and effectively communicating insights to various stakeholders within an organization. Studying managerial accounting enhances individuals' communication skills, enabling them to present financial data in a clear and concise manner to non-financial professionals. This ability to collaborate and communicate with colleagues, team members, and executives is essential in managerial roles, where financial information needs to be effectively shared and understood.

7. **Entrepreneurial Skills:** Studying managerial accounting is beneficial for aspiring entrepreneurs and small business owners. It provides them with essential financial management skills to make informed decisions, analyze costs, determine pricing strategies, and assess the financial viability of their ventures. Managerial accounting equips individuals with the tools to understand financial statements,

manage cash flow, and evaluate the financial health of their businesses.

Studying managerial accounting offers valuable insights and skills for decision-making within organizations. It provides individuals with the ability to analyze costs, evaluate performance, plan strategically, and communicate financial information effectively. Whether pursuing a career in management, entrepreneurship, or any other field, managerial accounting knowledge is crucial for success. It enables individuals to navigate the financial complexities of organizations, make informed decisions, and contribute to their overall performance and growth.

C. Studying Tax Accounting

Studying tax accounting offers numerous benefits and opportunities for individuals interested in pursuing careers in accounting, finance, or related fields. Tax accounting is a specialized area that focuses on understanding and applying tax laws and regulations. Here are several compelling reasons why studying tax accounting is important:

1. **Compliance with Tax Laws:** Tax accounting enables individuals and businesses to comply with tax laws and regulations. By studying tax accounting, individuals gain knowledge about the tax code, tax planning strategies, and compliance requirements. This understanding is essential for accurately preparing tax returns, ensuring timely filing, and avoiding penalties or legal issues related to taxation.

2. **Cost Savings:** Understanding tax laws and regulations allows individuals and businesses to identify tax-saving opportunities and optimize their tax liability. By studying tax accounting, individuals can learn about various deductions, credits, and exemptions available under the tax code. This knowledge helps minimize tax burdens and maximize after-tax income, resulting in cost savings for individuals and businesses.

3. **Strategic Planning:** Tax accounting plays a vital role in strategic financial planning. By studying tax accounting, individuals gain insights into the tax implications of different financial decisions, such as investments, business expansions, or acquisitions. This knowledge helps individuals and businesses make informed decisions that align with their long-term goals while considering the tax consequences associated with those decisions.

4. **Business Compliance:** For businesses, tax accounting is crucial for complying with tax laws and regulations specific to their industry or location. By studying tax accounting, individuals gain an understanding of business tax requirements, such as sales tax, payroll tax, and corporate tax. This knowledge allows businesses to accurately report and remit taxes, ensuring compliance with tax regulations and minimizing the risk of audits or penalties.

5. **Career Opportunities:** Studying tax accounting opens up a wide range of career opportunities. Tax accountants are in demand in public accounting firms, corporate finance departments, government agencies, and consulting firms. By specializing in tax accounting, individuals can pursue careers as tax advisors, tax consultants, tax analysts, or tax managers. Tax accounting expertise is highly valued by organizations seeking professionals who can navigate complex tax laws and provide strategic tax planning advice.

6. **Personal Financial Management:** Tax accounting knowledge is not only valuable for businesses but also for individuals managing their personal finances. By studying tax accounting, individuals can understand the tax implications of their income, investments, and expenses. This knowledge allows them to make informed financial decisions that minimize their tax burden and maximize their personal financial well-being.

7. **Changing Tax Landscape:** Tax laws and regulations are subject to frequent changes and updates. Studying tax accounting ensures individuals stay informed about these changes and can adapt their tax strategies accordingly. This knowledge is crucial for individuals and businesses to remain compliant, take advantage of new tax incentives or credits, and navigate the evolving tax landscape.

Studying tax accounting offers numerous advantages and opportunities. It equips individuals with the knowledge and skills to comply with tax laws, optimize tax liabilities, and strategically plan their financial decisions. Whether pursuing a career in tax accounting or any other field, tax accounting knowledge is valuable for personal financial management, business compliance, and maximizing cost savings. Additionally, the demand for tax accounting professionals continues to grow, providing diverse career opportunities in various sectors.

D. Studying Auditing

Studying auditing offers numerous benefits and opportunities for individuals interested in pursuing careers in accounting, finance, or related fields. Auditing is a specialized area that focuses on examining and evaluating financial records to provide an independent assessment of an organization's financial statements. Here are several compelling reasons why studying auditing is important:

1. **Assurance and Confidence:** Auditing plays a critical role in providing assurance and enhancing confidence in financial reporting. By studying auditing, individuals learn the principles and techniques necessary to examine financial records, assess internal controls, and verify the accuracy and reliability of financial statements. This knowledge helps instill trust in financial information among stakeholders, including investors, lenders, regulators, and the general public.

2. **Compliance and Risk Management:** Auditing assists organizations in complying with legal and regulatory requirements. By studying auditing, individuals gain knowledge about auditing standards, regulations, and governance frameworks. This understanding enables them to assess the organization's compliance with applicable laws and regulations and identify potential areas of risk or non-compliance. Auditors help organizations mitigate risks by providing recommendations for improvement in internal controls and operational processes.

3. **Corporate Governance:** Auditing is closely linked to corporate governance, which encompasses the systems and processes by which companies are directed and controlled. By studying auditing, individuals gain insights into the role of auditors in promoting transparency, accountability, and ethical conduct within organizations. Auditors provide an independent and objective assessment of an organization's financial operations, ensuring that management acts in the best interests of shareholders and stakeholders.

4. **Professional Skepticism and Critical Thinking:** Auditing develops individuals' professional skepticism and critical thinking abilities. By studying auditing, individuals learn to approach financial information with a questioning mindset, critically evaluate evidence, and identify potential errors, fraud, or misstatements. These skills are invaluable in various professional roles, enabling individuals to

analyze complex data, identify patterns, and draw logical conclusions.

5. **Career Opportunities:** Studying auditing opens up diverse career opportunities. Auditors are in demand in public accounting firms, corporations, government agencies, and non-profit organizations. By specializing in auditing, individuals can pursue careers as external auditors, internal auditors, forensic auditors, or compliance officers. Auditing expertise is highly valued by organizations seeking professionals who can assess financial integrity, identify risks, and provide recommendations for improvement.

6. **Professional Development and Credibility:** Studying auditing enhances professional development and credibility. Auditing requires a strong knowledge of accounting principles, financial reporting standards, and auditing procedures. By studying auditing, individuals gain expertise in these areas and demonstrate their commitment to high professional standards. This knowledge and credibility can lead to increased career opportunities, promotions, and recognition within the accounting and finance profession.

7. **Continuous Learning and Adaptability:** Auditing is a field that continuously evolves in response to changing business practices, technologies, and regulations. By studying auditing, individuals develop a mindset of continuous learning and adaptability. They stay updated with emerging

auditing techniques, technology-driven audit procedures, and evolving regulatory requirements. This ability to adapt and learn ensures that auditors remain relevant and effective in their roles.

Studying auditing offers numerous advantages and opportunities. It equips individuals with the knowledge and skills to provide assurance, enhance corporate governance, ensure compliance, and mitigate risks. Whether pursuing a career in auditing or any other field, auditing knowledge is valuable for critical thinking, professional development, and building credibility. Additionally, the demand for auditing professionals continues to grow, providing diverse career opportunities in various sectors.

E. Studying Governmental and Nonprofit Accounting
Studying governmental and nonprofit accounting offers numerous benefits and opportunities for individuals interested in pursuing careers in accounting, finance, or related fields within the public and nonprofit sectors. Governmental and nonprofit organizations have unique accounting and financial reporting requirements that differ from those of for-profit entities. Here are several compelling reasons why studying governmental and nonprofit accounting is important:

1. **Understanding Specific Accounting Standards:** Governmental and nonprofit organizations follow specialized accounting standards and frameworks tailored to their unique needs. By studying governmental and nonprofit accounting, individuals gain knowledge of these specific standards, such as the Governmental Accounting Standards Board

(GASB) for governmental entities and the Financial Accounting Standards Board (FASB) for nonprofit organizations. This understanding enables individuals to navigate the complexities of financial reporting in these sectors and ensures compliance with the applicable accounting principles.

2. **Fulfilling Public Service Mission:** Governmental and nonprofit organizations have a primary objective of serving the public interest rather than generating profits. By studying governmental and nonprofit accounting, individuals develop an understanding of the financial management practices specific to these organizations. This knowledge allows individuals to contribute to the effective stewardship of public resources and the achievement of the organization's mission and objectives.

3. **Budgeting and Fiscal Control:** Governmental and nonprofit accounting emphasizes budgeting and fiscal control. These organizations often operate within budget constraints and are accountable for the responsible use of public or donor funds. By studying governmental and nonprofit accounting, individuals gain skills in budget development, expenditure control, and performance monitoring. This knowledge enables effective financial management, promotes transparency, and ensures accountability in the allocation and utilization of resources.

4. **Grant and Fund Accounting:** Governmental and nonprofit organizations often rely on grants, donations, and restricted funds to finance their

activities. Studying governmental and nonprofit accounting provides individuals with the understanding of grant and fund accounting principles. This knowledge is essential for tracking and reporting on the use of restricted funds, complying with grant requirements, and ensuring proper stewardship of donor contributions.

5. **Compliance with Regulatory Requirements:** Governmental and nonprofit organizations must adhere to specific regulatory requirements, including tax-exempt status, reporting to government agencies, and compliance with funding restrictions. By studying governmental and nonprofit accounting, individuals gain knowledge of these regulatory frameworks and reporting obligations. This understanding enables organizations to meet their legal and regulatory responsibilities and maintain their tax-exempt status.

6. **Career Opportunities:** Studying governmental and nonprofit accounting opens up diverse career opportunities in public sector agencies, nonprofit organizations, and consulting firms that specialize in these sectors. Individuals with expertise in governmental and nonprofit accounting are in demand for roles such as auditors, financial analysts, budget managers, and controllers. The public and nonprofit sectors offer meaningful work experiences and opportunities to contribute to the well-being of communities and society as a whole.

7. **Ethical Considerations:** Governmental and nonprofit accounting often involves handling public funds or donor contributions, which requires a high level of ethical responsibility. By studying governmental and nonprofit accounting, individuals develop an understanding of the ethical considerations specific to these sectors. This knowledge helps individuals make sound ethical decisions and ensures the proper use and reporting of public or donor funds.

Studying governmental and nonprofit accounting offers numerous advantages and opportunities. It equips individuals with the knowledge and skills to navigate the unique financial reporting requirements of these sectors, contribute to effective resource management, and fulfill the public service mission of organizations. Whether pursuing a career in the public sector or nonprofit organizations, studying governmental and nonprofit accounting is crucial for understanding the complexities of financial management and ensuring compliance with regulatory requirements. Additionally, the demand for professionals with expertise in governmental and nonprofit accounting continues to grow, providing diverse career opportunities in these sectors.

CHAPTER TWO
What is Financial Accounting?

Financial accounting is a specialized branch of accounting that focuses on the recording, summarizing, and reporting of financial transactions and information of an organization. Its primary purpose is to provide relevant and reliable financial information to external users, such as investors, creditors, regulatory authorities, and other stakeholders, for decision-making purposes. At its core, financial accounting aims to capture and communicate the financial performance and position of a business entity. It involves the systematic recording of financial transactions, classifying them into various categories, and summarizing them in financial statements. These financial statements, including the balance sheet, income statement, statement of cash flows, and statement of changes in equity, provide a comprehensive view of the organization's financial health and performance over a specific period.

One of the key principles of financial accounting is the adherence to generally accepted accounting principles (GAAP) or international financial reporting standards (IFRS). These sets of rules and guidelines ensure consistency, comparability, and transparency in financial reporting across different entities and jurisdictions. By following these standards, financial accountants ensure that the information presented in the financial statements is reliable, understandable, and useful to the intended users. Financial accounting involves the use of various techniques and concepts to measure and record financial transactions accurately. These include double-entry bookkeeping, which ensures that every transaction has equal debits and credits, and accrual accounting, which recognizes revenues and expenses when they are earned or incurred, rather than when cash is exchanged. Other concepts such as historical cost, materiality, and conservatism also play a role in financial accounting.

Financial accounting provides valuable information for decision-making purposes. Investors use financial statements to assess the profitability and financial stability of a company before making investment decisions. Creditors evaluate financial statements to determine the creditworthiness and repayment capacity of a borrower. Regulatory authorities rely on financial statements to monitor compliance with laws and regulations. In addition to external users, financial accounting also serves internal users within an organization. Management utilizes financial reports to analyze financial performance, assess the efficiency of operations, and make informed decisions about resource allocation, cost control, and strategic planning. Financial ratios, trend analysis, and other financial tools help management evaluate performance and identify areas for improvement.

Financial accounting is a crucial component of the overall accounting discipline. It plays a vital role in capturing and communicating the financial information of an organization to external users for decision-making purposes. By following accounting standards and principles, financial accountants ensure the accuracy, reliability, and comparability of financial statements. Through its reports and analysis, financial accounting enables stakeholders to assess the financial health and performance of a company, make informed investment decisions, and ensure regulatory compliance.

The Five Classifications of Financial Accounting

In financial accounting, the areas typically refer to the five main categories of accounts used to record financial transactions. These classifications are also known as the five types of accounts or the five elements of accounting. They are:

1. **Assets:** Assets are economic resources owned or controlled by an entity that have measurable value and are expected to provide future economic benefits. Examples of assets include cash, accounts receivable, inventory, property, plant, and equipment.

2. **Liabilities:** Liabilities are obligations or debts owed by an entity to external parties. They represent the claims against the assets of the entity. Examples of liabilities include accounts payable, loans payable, accrued expenses, and bonds payable.

3. **Equity:** Equity represents the residual interest in the assets of an entity after deducting liabilities. It represents the ownership interest of the owners or shareholders. It includes share capital, retained earnings, and other equity accounts.

4. **Revenue:** Revenue refers to the inflow of economic benefits resulting from the ordinary activities of an entity. It is generated from the sale of goods,

provision of services, or other business activities. Revenue is typically recorded when it is earned and realizable.

5. **Expenses:** Expenses are the costs incurred in the process of generating revenue or maintaining the operations of an entity. They represent the outflow of economic benefits. Examples of expenses include salaries and wages, rent, utilities, depreciation, and advertising expenses.

These areas form the foundation of financial accounting. They provide a systematic way to record, summarize, and present financial information in financial statements, such as the balance sheet, income statement, and statement of cash flows.

Common Current Assets

1. *Cash and Cash Equivalents:* This includes physical currency, such as coins and banknotes, as well as funds held in checking accounts, savings accounts, and short-term investments that can be easily converted to cash. Cash equivalents are highly liquid investments with a maturity date within three months from the date of acquisition.

2. *Accounts Receivable:* These represent amounts owed to a business by its customers or clients for goods sold or services rendered on credit. Accounts receivable arise from sales made on credit terms, and they are expected to be collected within a short

period, typically 30 to 90 days. They are considered an asset as they represent future cash inflows.

3. *Inventory:* Inventory consists of goods held for sale in the normal course of business or materials and supplies used in the production process. It includes raw materials, work-in-progress, and finished goods. Inventory is valued at the lower of cost or net realizable value and is an important asset for businesses involved in manufacturing, wholesale, or retail operations.

4. *Prepaid Expenses:* Prepaid expenses are payments made in advance for goods or services that will be received in the future. Examples include prepaid rent, prepaid insurance premiums, prepaid advertising expenses, and prepaid subscriptions. Prepaid expenses are initially recorded as assets and are gradually recognized as expenses over the periods to which they relate.

5. *Short-term Investments:* These are investments that a company plans to hold for a relatively short period, typically less than one year. Short-term investments include marketable securities, such as Treasury bills, commercial paper, and certificates of deposit. They are considered liquid assets that can be readily converted into cash if needed.

6. *Marketable Securities:* These are highly liquid investments that can be easily bought or sold in the financial markets. Marketable securities include stocks, bonds, and other debt securities that a

company holds as investments. They are classified as current assets if they have a maturity date of less than one year.

Current assets are vital to a company's liquidity and operational cycle. They represent resources that are expected to be converted into cash or used up within a short period, usually one year or less. These assets enable businesses to meet their short-term obligations, such as paying for operating expenses, salaries, and other liabilities. Effective management of current assets is essential for maintaining cash flow, funding day-to-day operations, and ensuring the financial stability of a company.

Here are examples of each current asset:

1. **Cash and Cash Equivalents:**
   - Physical currency (coins and banknotes)
   - Cash held in checking accounts
   - Cash held in savings accounts
   - Petty cash on hand
   - Money market funds
   - Highly liquid short-term investments

2. **Accounts Receivable:**
   - Amounts owed by customers for goods sold or services rendered on credit
   - Outstanding invoices or bills receivable
   - Trade receivables from business-to-business transactions
   - Notes receivable

3. **Inventory:**
   - Raw materials used in production
   - Work-in-progress (partially completed products)
   - Finished goods ready for sale
   - Merchandise held by retailers or wholesalers
   - Spare parts or components
   - Supplies for internal use (office supplies, cleaning materials, etc.)

4. **Prepaid Expenses:**
   - Prepaid rent for office space or facilities
   - Prepaid insurance premiums
   - Prepaid advertising expenses
   - Prepaid maintenance or service contracts
   - Prepaid subscriptions (e.g., magazines, software licenses)

5. **Short-term Investments:**
   - Treasury bills (T-bills)
   - Certificates of deposit (CDs)
   - Commercial paper
   - Money market funds
   - Government bonds with a maturity of less than one year

6. **Marketable Securities:**
   - Stocks or shares of publicly traded companies
   - Corporate bonds with a maturity of less than one year

- Treasury bills (T-bills) with a maturity of less than one year
- Mutual funds with high liquidity

These examples represent the common types of current assets that businesses may have on their balance sheets. It's important to note that the specific assets held by a company can vary depending on its industry, nature of operations, and individual circumstances.

Common Fixed Assets

Fixed assets are recorded on the balance sheet at their historical cost, which includes the purchase price and any associated costs incurred to bring the asset into its intended use. Over time, fixed assets are systematically depreciated using various depreciation methods, such as straight-line, declining balance, or units of production, to allocate the cost of the asset over its estimated useful life.

Fixed assets are important to a business as they contribute to its revenue generation and operational efficiency. They enable the production of goods or provision of services, and their proper management is crucial for optimizing productivity, maintaining the value of assets, and ensuring compliance with accounting standards and regulations. Fixed assets, also known as property, plant, and equipment (PP&E), are long-term tangible assets held by a business that are used in its operations to generate revenue. These assets are not intended for sale or conversion into cash within a short period.

Common Types of Fixed Assets:

1. *Land:* Land represents the value of the company's property or real estate holdings. It includes the cost of the land itself, as well as any associated costs such as legal fees, site preparation, and improvements to the land.

2. *Buildings:* Buildings refer to structures owned or used by the business for its operations. This includes office buildings, factories, warehouses, retail stores, and other facilities. The cost of buildings includes the purchase price, construction costs, renovations, and improvements.

3. *Machinery and Equipment:* This category encompasses a wide range of assets used in the production or manufacturing process. It includes machinery, tools, vehicles, computers, furniture, fixtures, and any other tangible assets utilized to support the business operations. These assets are generally subject to depreciation over their estimated useful lives.

4. *Vehicles:* Vehicles represent automobiles, trucks, vans, or other modes of transportation used in business activities. These assets are typically used for deliveries, transportation of goods, or as part of the company's service operations.

5. *Furniture and Fixtures:* Furniture and fixtures refer to items such as desks, chairs, shelves, cabinets, lighting fixtures, and other furnishings used in business premises. These assets contribute to the functionality and aesthetics of the workspace.

6. *Accumulated Depreciation:* Accumulated depreciation is not a separate fixed asset but rather a contra-asset account that represents the total depreciation recognized on the fixed assets. It reflects the decrease in the value of fixed assets over time due to wear and tear, obsolescence, or the passage of time. Accumulated depreciation is subtracted from the historical cost of the fixed asset to determine its net book value.

Common Types of Investments

Investments are recorded on the balance sheet at their fair value, which may be based on market prices or estimated values. The specific classification and accounting treatment of investments depend on factors such as the purpose of the investment, the business's intention, and applicable accounting standards. Investments play a crucial role in diversifying a company's asset portfolio, generating returns, and achieving financial objectives.

1. *Long-term Investments:* Long-term investments are assets held by a business with the intention of generating income or capital appreciation over an extended period, typically more than one year. These investments are not readily convertible into cash and

are not intended for sale in the short term. Examples of long-term investments include:

a. **Equity Investments:** These are investments in the ownership shares of other companies, such as stocks or shares of publicly traded companies. The business holds these investments with the expectation of earning dividends or capital gains.

b. **Bonds and Notes Receivable:** Bonds and notes receivable represent loans made by the business to other entities. These investments typically involve the lending of funds in exchange for regular interest payments and the return of principal at maturity.

c. **Mutual Funds:** Mutual funds pool money from multiple investors to invest in a diversified portfolio of securities, such as stocks, bonds, or other financial instruments. Businesses may invest in mutual funds to benefit from professional portfolio management and diversification.

d. **Real Estate Investments:** These investments involve the acquisition and ownership of properties, such as residential, commercial, or industrial real estate, with the goal of generating rental income or capital appreciation.

2. ***Equity Investments:*** Equity investments represent ownership stakes in other companies. These investments can be classified into two main categories:

- Strategic Investments: Strategic investments are made in companies that have a significant impact on the investing company's operations, markets, or strategic direction. The investing company typically acquires a substantial ownership stake and may have the ability to influence the investee's decisions.

- Passive Investments: Passive equity investments refer to minority stakes in other companies where the investing company does not have significant control or influence over the investee's operations or decision-making.

3. ***Bonds and Fixed-Income Securities:*** Bonds and fixed-income securities are debt instruments issued by governments, municipalities, corporations, or other entities to raise capital. When a business invests in bonds, it essentially lends money to the issuer in exchange for periodic interest payments and the repayment of the principal amount at maturity.

4. ***Money Market Instruments:*** Money market instruments are short-term, highly liquid investments with a maturity period of one year or less. These investments include Treasury bills, commercial paper, certificates of deposit (CDs), and other low-

risk instruments. They provide a means for businesses to invest excess cash and earn interest while maintaining liquidity.

5. *Derivatives:* Derivatives are financial instruments whose value is derived from an underlying asset, such as stocks, bonds, commodities, or currencies. Common types of derivatives include options, futures contracts, and swaps. Businesses may use derivatives for various purposes, including hedging against price fluctuations, managing risks, or speculating on market movements.

Common Types of Intangible Assets

Intangible assets are crucial for businesses as they often contribute significantly to their competitive advantage and value. While intangible assets lack physical substance, they can generate substantial revenue, enhance brand equity, and support long-term growth. These assets are recorded on the balance sheet at their fair value, typically acquired through purchase or development. Intangible assets may be subject to amortization (for finite-lived assets) or impairment testing to reflect their value accurately over time. Proper management and protection of intangible assets are essential for preserving a company's intellectual property and maximizing their potential value.

1. *Goodwill:* Goodwill represents the value of a business's reputation, customer relationships, brand recognition, and other intangible factors that contribute to its market position and earning

potential. Goodwill arises when a company acquires another company for a price higher than the fair value of its identifiable net assets. Goodwill is recorded on the balance sheet and is subject to periodic impairment testing.

2. *Patents:* Patents provide exclusive rights to an inventor or a company for a specified period, typically 20 years, to protect their inventions or discoveries. They grant the patent holder the sole right to produce, use, or sell the patented product or process. Patents are valuable assets that can generate revenue through licensing or by preventing competitors from using the patented technology.

3. *Trademarks:* Trademarks are distinctive signs, symbols, logos, or names that represent a company's products or services. They serve to differentiate a business from its competitors and create brand recognition among consumers. Trademarks can be registered with the appropriate government authority to protect their exclusive use by the owner.

4. *Copyrights:* Copyrights protect original works of authorship, such as literature, music, artwork, software code, or architectural designs. They grant the creator or owner the exclusive right to reproduce, distribute, display, or perform the copyrighted work. Copyrights provide legal protection against unauthorized use and allow the owner to monetize their intellectual property.

5. ***Brand Value:*** Brand value encompasses the intangible worth associated with a company's brand name, reputation, customer loyalty, and market recognition. A strong brand can command premium pricing, increase customer trust, and contribute to the long-term success and profitability of a business.

6. ***Software:*** Software represents computer programs and applications developed by a company for its internal use or for sale to customers. Software can be considered an intangible asset if it is identifiable, has a determinable useful life, and provides future economic benefits. Examples include proprietary software, customized applications, and software licenses.

Common Types of "Other" Assets

"Other assets" is a broad category that encompasses various types of assets that don't fit into the conventional classifications of current assets, fixed assets, or intangible assets. These assets are typically less common or specific to certain industries. Here are some examples and explanations of other assets:

1. ***Long-term Investments:*** While long-term investments are sometimes categorized separately, they can also be included as part of "other assets." Long-term investments are assets held by a business for more than one year with the expectation of generating income or capital appreciation. Examples include equity investments in other companies, bonds, mutual funds, and real estate investments.

2. **Deferred Charges:** Deferred charges refer to costs incurred by a business that will be expensed over multiple accounting periods rather than in the period when they were incurred. These costs represent future benefits and are recorded as assets until they are recognized as expenses. Examples include deferred financing costs, deferred advertising costs, and deferred research and development expenses.

3. **Non-current Receivables:** Non-current receivables are amounts owed to a business that are not expected to be collected within the next year. These receivables have a longer payment term and are classified as non-current assets. Examples include long-term loans receivable, installment sales receivables, and non-current trade receivables.

4. **Deposits:** Deposits represent funds or assets held by a business as a security or guarantee for future transactions or obligations. These assets are typically refundable or recoverable upon fulfilling specific conditions. Examples of deposits include rental or lease deposits, utility deposits, and customer or vendor deposits.

5. **Deferred Tax Assets:** Deferred tax assets arise when a business has overpaid taxes or has accumulated tax benefits that can be utilized to offset future taxable income. These assets represent the potential tax savings that can be realized in future periods. Examples include tax loss carryforwards, tax credits, and deductible temporary differences.

6. **Restricted Cash:** Restricted cash refers to funds that are not freely available for general use by the business. These funds are typically held in a separate account and can only be used for specific purposes or under certain conditions. Examples of restricted cash include escrow accounts, security deposits, and funds held for regulatory compliance or contractual obligations.

It's important to note that the classification and terminology of other assets may vary depending on accounting standards and specific business circumstances. These assets are typically disclosed separately on the balance sheet to provide transparency and clarity regarding the company's asset composition.

The Accounting Cycle

The accounting cycle is a series of steps that accountants follow to record, classify, summarize, and analyze financial transactions. It is a systematic process that ensures the accuracy and reliability of financial information. This chapter provides an overview of the accounting cycle and explains each step-in detail.

Steps of the Accounting Cycle:

1. **Analyzing Transactions:** The first step in the accounting cycle is to analyze and identify the financial transactions that have occurred. Accountants examine source documents such as

invoices, receipts, and bank statements to understand the nature of each transaction.

2. *Recording Journal Entries:* Once the transactions are analyzed, accountants record journal entries. Journal entries capture the double-entry bookkeeping system, where each transaction is recorded with equal debits and credits, ensuring that the accounting equation remains balanced.

3. *Posting to the General Ledger:* After journal entries are recorded, the next step is to post them to the general ledger. The general ledger contains individual accounts for each asset, liability, equity, revenue, and expense. Posting transfers, the information from the journal to the respective accounts in the general ledger.

4. *Preparing a Trial Balance:* A trial balance is prepared to ensure the equality of debits and credits. It lists all the account balances from the general ledger and helps identify any errors or discrepancies in the recording or posting process.

5. *Adjusting Entries:* Adjusting entries are made at the end of the accounting period to reflect accrued revenues, expenses, prepaid expenses, and unearned revenues. These entries ensure that the financial statements reflect the proper recognition of revenues and expenses.

6. *Preparing Financial Statements:* Once the adjusting entries are made, the financial statements can be prepared. The main financial statements include the income statement, balance sheet, statement of cash flows, and statement of changes in equity. These statements provide a snapshot of the company's financial performance, position, cash flows, and changes in equity.

7. *Closing Entries:* Closing entries are made at the end of the accounting period to transfer the temporary accounts' balances (revenue, expense, and dividend accounts) to the retained earnings account. This process resets the temporary accounts to zero and prepares them for the next accounting period.

8. *Post-Closing Trial Balance:* After the closing entries are made, a post-closing trial balance is prepared. It ensures that all temporary accounts have been properly closed and that the balance sheet accounts reflect accurate ending balances.

Importance of the Accounting Cycle:

Mastering Financial Accounting: A Comprehensive Guide for Accountants and Business Students" examine the accounting cycle, highlighting its importance and the steps involved. The accounting cycle ensures the accuracy, reliability, and compliance of financial information. By following these steps, accountants can generate meaningful financial statements that assist in decision-making, provide transparency, and support accountability. A thorough understanding of the accounting cycle is crucial for individuals pursuing careers in accounting and finance.

The accounting cycle is essential for several reasons:

1. *Accuracy and Reliability:* Following the accounting cycle ensures that financial information is accurately recorded, classified, and summarized. This improves the reliability of the financial statements and provides users with trustworthy information for decision-making.

2. *Compliance:* The accounting cycle helps ensure compliance with accounting principles, standards, and regulations. By following the prescribed steps, organizations can demonstrate adherence to accounting requirements and maintain transparency in their financial reporting.

3. *Decision-Making:* The accounting cycle provides timely and relevant financial information that supports informed decision-making. The financial statements derived from the accounting cycle help stakeholders assess the financial health, profitability, and cash flow of a company, enabling them to make sound business decisions.

4. *Auditing and Accountability:* The accounting cycle creates an audit trail that facilitates external audits. The systematic recording of transactions, proper documentation, and adherence to the accounting cycle enable auditors to verify the accuracy of financial statements and ensure accountability.

5. *Financial Analysis:* The accounting cycle produces financial statements that serve as the foundation for financial analysis. Analysts and investors use these statements to assess the company's performance, profitability, and financial stability.

CHAPTER THREE
What is a Source Document?

Source documents are the original records or evidence that provide details about a business transaction. They serve as the foundation of the accounting process, providing essential information for recording and validating financial transactions. Source documents play a crucial role in ensuring the accuracy, reliability, and integrity of a company's financial records. Here's an in-depth look at source documents and their importance in financial accounting.

Examples of Source documents are physical or electronic records that capture key information about a business transaction. They provide evidence of the transaction's occurrence, the parties involved, the amounts involved, and any relevant supporting details. These documents can take various forms depending on the nature of the transaction and the industry, but they commonly include:

1. **Invoices:** Issued by a supplier to the company for the purchase of goods or services. Invoices typically include details such as the date, description of the items purchased, quantities, unit prices, terms of payment, and total amount due.

2. **Receipts:** Provided by the company to customers as proof of payment received for goods or services. Receipts usually contain information such as the date, customer name, description of the items or services, payment method, and amount paid.

3. **Purchase Orders:** Generated by the company to request the purchase of goods or services from a supplier. Purchase orders specify the items or services required, quantities, agreed-upon prices, delivery terms, and other relevant terms and conditions.

4. **Sales Orders:** Received by the company from customers, indicating their intention to purchase goods or services. Sales orders typically include details such as the customer's name, requested items, quantities, agreed prices, delivery instructions, and any special terms or conditions.

5. **Bank Statements:** Provided by the bank, they show the company's transactions, including deposits, withdrawals, checks issued or received, electronic transfers, and bank charges or fees.

6. **Payroll Records:** Documenting employee compensation, including wage rates, hours worked, deductions, benefits, and taxes withheld.

7. **Contracts and Agreements:** Formal documents outlining the terms and conditions of business transactions, such as lease agreements, loan agreements, purchase agreements, and employment contracts.

Significance of Source Documents

In the world of business, accurate and reliable recordkeeping is crucial for maintaining financial transparency, complying with legal requirements, and facilitating efficient operations. At the heart of this process lie source documents, the foundation upon which a company's financial records are built. In this book, we will explore the importance of source documents, their various types, and how they contribute to effective recordkeeping.

One of the key benefits of source documents is their ability to provide an audit trail. By preserving evidence of each transaction, they enable businesses to trace the flow of financial information, verify the accuracy of entries, and resolve any discrepancies that may arise. This is particularly important during audits, as source documents help external auditors assess the reliability of a company's financial statements.

Source documents are original records that serve as evidence of business transactions. They provide the necessary details and documentation to support the preparation of accounting entries, financial statements, and tax returns. These documents play a fundamental role in ensuring the accuracy, integrity, and reliability of a company's financial records.

1. **Accuracy and Reliability:** Source documents ensure the accuracy and reliability of financial records. They provide the original information about a transaction, reducing the risk of errors, omissions, or unauthorized changes. By relying on source documents, accountants can record transactions

accurately, preventing discrepancies and ensuring that the financial statements reflect the true financial position of the company.

2. **Audit Trail and Verification:** Source documents create an audit trail, allowing transactions to be traced from their origin to the final financial statements. This traceability is vital for internal and external auditors, as it enables them to verify the accuracy and completeness of financial records. Auditors can examine source documents to validate transactions and ensure compliance with accounting principles and regulatory requirements.

3. **Legal and Regulatory Compliance:** Source documents play a crucial role in legal and regulatory compliance. They provide evidence of business transactions, supporting the preparation of tax returns, financial statements, and other reports required by regulatory authorities. Source documents demonstrate the company's adherence to laws, regulations, and contractual obligations, reducing the risk of penalties, fines, or legal disputes.

4. **Decision-Making Support:** Source documents provide valuable information for decision-making. Business owners, managers, and stakeholders rely on accurate and timely financial information to make informed decisions. Source documents supply the data necessary for analyzing costs, revenues, and profitability, evaluating investment opportunities, and assessing the financial health of the company.

5. **Internal Controls and Fraud Prevention:** Source documents contribute to internal controls and fraud prevention within an organization. They provide a basis for verifying transactions and detecting irregularities or potentially fraudulent activities. By ensuring that transactions are supported by appropriate source documents, companies can implement robust internal control systems and safeguard their assets.

6. **Financial Analysis and Planning:** Source documents are essential for financial analysis and planning. They enable financial analysts to analyze trends, calculate ratios, and perform other analytical techniques to evaluate the company's performance and identify areas for improvement. Source documents also support budgeting and forecasting processes by providing accurate and detailed information about past transactions and financial activities.

7. **Business Documentation and Communication:** Source documents serve as important business documentation and facilitate communication with stakeholders. They provide a clear and complete record of transactions, helping to resolve disputes, negotiate contracts, and maintain effective relationships with suppliers, customers, and financial institutions.

In addition to these specific types, source documents can also include items such as time sheets, payroll records, inventory records, shipping documents, and expense reports. Each of these documents captures important details related to various business activities, forming an essential part of the recordkeeping process.

Effective management and organization of source documents are critical for businesses to maintain accurate financial records. Proper filing, indexing, and storage systems ensure easy retrieval and access to the necessary information when required. Digitization has significantly enhanced this process, allowing for efficient electronic storage, quick search capabilities, and reduced physical storage needs.

Furthermore, source documents are subject to record retention requirements, which vary depending on the type of document and applicable regulations. It is essential for businesses to establish and adhere to a records retention policy to ensure compliance and avoid legal and financial risks.

Source documents form the bedrock of effective recordkeeping in business. They provide evidence of financial transactions, support the preparation of financial records, and enable accurate reporting. By preserving a trail of each transaction, these documents contribute to financial transparency, facilitate audits, and ensure compliance with legal requirements. Source documents are vital to the financial accounting process. They serve as the original records or evidence of business transactions, ensuring accuracy, reliability, compliance, and transparency in financial reporting. By relying on source documents, companies can maintain accurate financial records, support decision-making, comply with legal and regulatory requirements, implement internal controls, and provide a solid foundation for financial analysis and planning.

CHAPTER FOUR
What are Journal Entries?

Journal entries are a fundamental aspect of financial accounting that involve recording and documenting business transactions. They serve as a chronological record of these transactions, capturing the details of each event in a standardized format. Journal entries play a crucial role in maintaining accurate financial records and generating reliable financial statements. Here's an in-depth look at journal entries and their importance in financial accounting.

What are Journal Entries? Journal entries are the first step in the accounting process. They represent the initial recording of financial transactions in the general journal, which is a book or electronic system used to organize and store these entries. Each journal entry follows a consistent format, including the date, accounts involved, a brief description of the transaction, and the amounts debited and credited.

Journal entries adhere to the principles of double-entry bookkeeping, which means that every transaction has an equal debit and credit amount. This is based on the accounting equation: Assets = Liabilities + Owner's Equity. Journal entries ensure that this equation remains in balance and that every transaction is properly recorded.

Importance of Journal Entries:

1. **Accurate Financial Reporting:** Journal entries provide the foundation for accurate financial reporting. They capture the details of each

transaction, including the accounts affected and the corresponding amounts. By recording transactions promptly and accurately, journal entries ensure that financial statements reflect the true financial position and performance of the business.

2. **Complete Audit Trail:** Journal entries serve as an audit trail, providing a clear record of all financial transactions. This trail is essential for internal and external auditors to verify the accuracy and integrity of the company's financial records. It enables auditors to trace the flow of transactions from the initial entry to the final financial statements.

3. **Facilitate Financial Analysis:** Journal entries play a vital role in financial analysis. They provide the necessary data for calculating financial ratios, conducting trend analysis, and performing other analytical techniques. By having well-documented and accurate journal entries, financial analysts can make informed decisions and assess the financial health and performance of the business.

4. **Compliance with Accounting Standards:** Journal entries ensure compliance with accounting standards and regulations. Properly recorded journal entries help ensure that financial statements adhere to Generally Accepted Accounting Principles (GAAP) or International Financial Reporting Standards (IFRS). They provide transparency and comparability in financial reporting, allowing stakeholders to make meaningful comparisons across companies and industries.

5. **Efficient Bookkeeping:** Journal entries streamline the bookkeeping process. By systematically recording transactions, they create a chronological record that facilitates the organization and retrieval of financial information. Journal entries make it easier to identify and correct errors, reconcile accounts, and generate accurate financial statements in a timely manner.

6. **Decision-Making Support:** Journal entries provide valuable information for decision-making. By accurately recording transactions, they capture the financial impact of business activities. This data helps management analyze costs, revenues, and expenses, assess the profitability of specific projects or products, and make informed decisions to improve operational efficiency and financial performance.

7. **Legal and Regulatory Compliance:** Journal entries are crucial for legal and regulatory compliance. They serve as evidence of financial transactions and support the preparation of tax returns, financial statements, and other reports required by regulatory authorities. Journal entries provide transparency and accountability, helping businesses meet their legal obligations and avoid penalties or legal disputes.

8. **Internal Controls and Fraud Prevention:** Journal entries contribute to internal controls and fraud prevention within an organization. They ensure that transactions are properly authorized, recorded accurately, and supported by appropriate

documentation. Journal entries enable the detection of errors, irregularities, or potentially fraudulent activities, enhancing the company's internal control environment and safeguarding its assets.

In the field of accounting, journal entries play a vital role in recording and organizing financial transactions. These entries serve as the foundation for the double-entry bookkeeping system, ensuring accurate and reliable financial reporting. In this book, we will explore the purpose of journal entries, their components, and their significance in maintaining clear and comprehensive accounting records.

The primary purpose of journal entries is to record the effects of financial transactions on a company's accounts. Every time a business engages in a transaction, such as a sale, purchase, payment, or receipt of funds, a journal entry is created to document the specific details and ensure that the transaction is properly recorded. Journal entries capture the essential information needed to update the company's general ledger, which contains all the accounts used in its accounting system.

A typical journal entry consists of several key components. Firstly, there is the date, which indicates the day on which the transaction occurred. The date helps in organizing and tracking transactions chronologically, making it easier to refer back to specific events. Secondly, there is the account title, which identifies the account that is being debited or credited. The account title corresponds to the various categories in the chart of accounts, such as cash, accounts receivable, inventory, or accounts payable.

Journal entries include a brief description of the transaction, providing additional context and clarity. This description should be concise but informative, explaining the nature of the transaction and the purpose behind it. For example, a journal entry for a sale transaction might include the name of the customer, the type of product sold, and the sale amount. Similarly, a journal entry for a payment to a supplier may include the supplier's name, the invoice number, and the payment method.

The debit and credit columns are crucial components of a journal entry. In double-entry bookkeeping, each transaction affects at least two accounts, with one account being debited and another being credited. The debit side represents an increase in assets or expenses, or a decrease in liabilities or equity. The credit side, on the other hand, signifies an increase in liabilities or equity, or a decrease in assets or expenses. The debits and credits must balance, ensuring that the accounting equation (Assets = Liabilities + Equity) remains in equilibrium.

The amounts recorded in the debit and credit columns of a journal entry are determined based on the specific transaction and the rules of accounting. For example, when a company receives cash from a customer for a sale, the cash account is debited to reflect the increase in cash, while the sales revenue account is credited to record the increase in revenue. Each journal entry must have equal total debits and credits, ensuring that the accounting equation is satisfied.

Journal entries are not only essential for recording day-to-day transactions but also for adjusting entries and closing entries. Adjusting entries are made at the end of an accounting period to ensure that revenues and expenses are recognized in the correct period. These entries help in accurately reflecting the company's financial position and performance. Closing entries, on the other hand, are made at the end of the accounting period to transfer temporary accounts (such as revenue and expense accounts) to the retained earnings account, preparing the accounts for the next period.

Maintaining accurate and complete journal entries is crucial for several reasons. Firstly, they provide a detailed record of financial transactions, enabling businesses to track and analyze their financial activities. Journal entries serve as evidence and support for the information presented in financial statements, making them essential for external audits and regulatory compliance. Additionally, they facilitate the preparation of financial reports, such as the balance sheet and income statement, which provide valuable insights into a company's financial health.

Journal entries are a fundamental aspect of accounting, serving as the primary means of recording financial transactions. They capture the necessary information, including dates, account titles, descriptions, and debit/credit amounts, ensuring the accuracy and integrity of a company's financial records. Journal entries not only provide a comprehensive overview of a business's financial activities but also contribute to the preparation of financial statements and support audit processes. Understanding the significance of journal entries and maintaining accurate records is essential for businesses to effectively manage their finances and make informed decisions.

Journal entries are a fundamental component of financial accounting. They provide a detailed record of financial transactions, ensure accurate financial reporting, support financial analysis and decision-making, facilitate compliance with accounting standards, and contribute to internal controls and fraud prevention.

The Purpose of T Accounts

The purpose of T accounts in financial accounting is to provide a visual representation and organization of the transactions and balances for specific accounts. T accounts are a tool used to analyze and record financial transactions in a structured and systematic manner. They are called T accounts because they are shaped like the letter "T," with a horizontal line representing the account title and vertical lines dividing the account into two sides.

The left side of the T account is referred to as the debit side, while the right side is known as the credit side. The debit side is typically used to record increases in assets and expenses and decreases in liabilities, equity, and revenues. The credit side, on the other hand, is used to record increases in liabilities, equity, and revenues and decreases in assets and expenses. The T account format helps to visually separate debits and credits and facilitates the understanding of the double-entry bookkeeping system.

The key purposes of T accounts in financial accounting include:

1. **Recording Transactions:** T accounts provide a clear and concise way to record and track the effects of financial transactions on specific accounts. Each transaction is analyzed and recorded as debits and credits in the respective T accounts, ensuring accurate and balanced entries.

2. **Visualizing Balances:** T accounts allow users to see the balances of specific accounts at a glance. The cumulative effect of all the debits and credits recorded in the T account provides a current balance for the account, helping to determine the financial position of the organization.

3. **Analyzing Account Activity:** T accounts help in analyzing the activity and changes in specific accounts over a period of time. By examining the debits and credits recorded in the T account, one can understand the inflows and outflows associated with the account and identify any trends or patterns.

4. **Facilitating Adjustments:** T accounts assist in making adjusting entries at the end of an accounting period. Adjusting entries, such as accruals or deferrals, can be easily recorded in the respective T accounts to reflect the proper recognition of revenue and expenses in the financial statements.

5. **Preparing Financial Statements:** T accounts serve as a basis for preparing financial statements. The balances and activity recorded in the T accounts are summarized and transferred to the financial statements, such as the income statement, balance sheet, and statement of cash flows.

6. **Supporting Auditing and Analysis:** T accounts provide a clear audit trail and support the examination of financial records. Auditors and financial analysts can review the T accounts to verify the accuracy and completeness of the recorded transactions and ensure compliance with accounting principles and regulations.

In the field of accounting, T accounts are a powerful tool used to visually represent the balances and transactions of various accounts. They serve as a fundamental component of the double-entry bookkeeping system and play a crucial role in understanding, analyzing, and summarizing financial information. In this book, we will explore the purpose of T accounts, their structure, and how they aid in financial analysis and decision-making.

The primary purpose of T accounts is to provide a clear and organized representation of the balances and transactions associated with specific accounts. Each T account consists of two sides: the left side, known as the debit side, and the right side, known as the credit side. The account title is written at the top of the T account, indicating the specific account being represented, such as cash, accounts receivable, inventory, or accounts payable.

T accounts serve as a visual aid to record and track the flow of debits and credits in each account. Debits are recorded on the left side of the T account, while credits are recorded on the right side. The balance of the account is determined by calculating the difference between the total debits and credits. If the total debits exceed the total credits, the account has a debit balance, while if the total credits exceed the total debits, the account has a credit balance.

T accounts are particularly useful for analyzing the impact of financial transactions on individual accounts and understanding their overall effect on the financial statements. By recording transactions in T accounts, accountants can easily identify the increases and decreases in specific accounts, providing a detailed record of the account's activity. This allows for accurate tracking of changes in assets, liabilities, equity, revenues, and expenses over time.

Furthermore, T accounts facilitate the preparation of trial balances, which are essential for ensuring the accuracy of financial records. A trial balance is a list of all the accounts in the general ledger, along with their respective debit and credit balances. By transferring the balances from the T accounts to the trial balance, accountants can verify that the total debits equal the total credits, thus ensuring that the accounting equation (Assets = Liabilities + Equity) is in balance.

T accounts also aid in financial analysis by providing a concise and organized summary of the transactions and balances of individual accounts. By examining the changes in the debit and credit sides of an account over a specific period, accountants can identify trends, patterns, and anomalies. This information is valuable for assessing the financial health of a company, identifying areas of improvement, and making informed decisions.

For example, by analyzing the T account for accounts receivable, a company can track the flow of sales, collections, and write-offs. This analysis provides insights into the effectiveness of the company's credit policies, the efficiency of its collection efforts, and the overall quality of its receivables. Similarly, by examining the T account for inventory, a company can monitor the purchases, sales, and adjustments made to its inventory levels, enabling effective inventory management and control.

T accounts also play a crucial role in financial statement preparation. They serve as the foundation for compiling the information needed to create the balance sheet, income statement, and statement of cash flows. By consolidating the balances from the T accounts, accountants can accurately determine the financial position, performance, and cash flow of a company.

In addition to their role in financial analysis and reporting, T accounts assist in decision-making processes. They provide a detailed record of transactions, allowing managers and stakeholders to evaluate the financial implications of various choices. By analyzing the T accounts, decision-makers can assess the potential impact on cash flow, profitability, and financial ratios, helping them make informed decisions that align with the company's goals and objectives.

T accounts serve a crucial purpose in accounting by providing a visual representation of the balances and transactions of individual accounts. They aid in understanding, analyzing, and summarizing financial information, ensuring accuracy and facilitating financial analysis and decision-making. T accounts are an essential tool in the double-entry bookkeeping system, enabling accountants to track the flow of debits and credits, prepare trial balances, and compile information for financial statement preparation. Understanding the purpose and structure of T accounts is essential for professionals in the field of accounting to effectively manage and interpret financial data.

T accounts serve as a fundamental tool in financial accounting, aiding in the recording, analysis, and reporting of financial transactions and balances. They provide a structured framework to maintain accurate and organized financial records, enabling users to understand the financial position and performance of an organization.

Recording Financial Transactions in a Journal

Recording financial transactions in a journal is important for several reasons:

1. **Chronological Order:** The journal provides a chronological record of all financial transactions, documenting them in the order in which they occur. This allows for a clear and organized representation of the transaction history, making it easier to track and understand the sequence of events.

2. **Audit Trail:** The journal serves as an audit trail or a source document for all financial transactions. It provides evidence of the transactions, including the date, description, and amounts involved. Having a complete and accurate journal helps auditors and accountants trace the flow of transactions and verify the accuracy of the financial records.

3. **Accuracy and Accountability:** By recording transactions in a journal, organizations ensure accuracy and accountability in their financial reporting. Each entry in the journal includes the specific accounts affected, the debits and credits, and supporting details. This detailed information helps prevent errors, misstatements, or fraudulent activities by providing a transparent record of the transaction.

4. **Reference for Future Use:** The journal acts as a reference tool for future use. It provides a historical record of financial transactions that can be referred to when preparing financial statements, analyzing

trends, or conducting financial analysis. The journal entries serve as a basis for creating reports and summaries of financial information.

5. **Facilitates the General Ledger:** The journal entries serve as the source for posting transactions to the general ledger. The general ledger is the central repository that contains all the accounts and their balances. By recording transactions in the journal, organizations can easily transfer the relevant information to the appropriate accounts in the general ledger, ensuring accurate and up-to-date financial information.

6. **Internal Control and Compliance:** Recording transactions in the journal helps establish internal control measures and ensures compliance with accounting principles and regulations. It enables organizations to maintain a systematic and standardized approach to recording and reporting financial transactions, reducing the risk of errors, omissions, or fraud.

7. **Historical Analysis:** The journal provides a historical record of financial transactions that can be analyzed for various purposes. It allows for the examination of past trends, patterns, and performance indicators. By reviewing the journal entries, organizations can gain insights into their financial activities and make informed decisions based on historical data.

Recording financial transactions in the journal is crucial for maintaining accurate financial records, providing an audit trail, ensuring accountability, facilitating the general ledger process, supporting compliance, and enabling historical analysis. It is an essential step in the accounting cycle and contributes to the overall integrity and reliability of an organization's financial information.

Before Performing Journal Entries

Performing journal entries is a critical step in the accounting process, as it allows businesses to record and track financial transactions accurately. However, before diving into the task of journalizing, there are several key considerations that need to be taken into account. In this book, we will explore the important steps and considerations to keep in mind before performing journal entries to ensure accurate and effective recordkeeping. Before performing journal entries, several steps should be taken to ensure accurate and complete recording of financial transactions. These steps include:

1. **Source Documents:** Collect and organize all relevant source documents such as invoices, receipts, purchase orders, bank statements, and other supporting documentation. These documents provide evidence of the transactions and serve as a reference for accurate journal entries.

2. **Transaction Analysis:** Analyze the nature of the transaction and determine the accounts and amounts involved. Identify the specific accounts that will be debited and credited based on the transaction details.

This analysis helps ensure that the journal entries accurately reflect the financial impact of the transaction.

3. **Account Classification:** Classify the accounts affected by the transaction. Determine whether the transaction relates to assets, liabilities, equity, revenues, or expenses. This step ensures that the journal entries are recorded in the appropriate accounts and comply with accounting principles and standards.

4. **Double-Entry Bookkeeping:** Apply the principle of double-entry bookkeeping. Every transaction should have at least two entries, with one debit and one credit. The total debits must equal the total credits to maintain the balance in the accounting equation.

5. **Recording Format:** Determine the format and structure for recording journal entries. This typically involves using a standardized journal format or software system that includes columns for date, account titles, debit amounts, credit amounts, and a brief description of the transaction.

6. **Consistency and Accuracy:** Ensure consistency and accuracy in recording the transactions. Follow the organization's established accounting policies, procedures, and chart of accounts. Verify the accuracy of numerical amounts and cross-check the debits and credits to avoid errors or imbalances.

7. **Review and Approval:** Review the journal entries before finalizing them. Perform a thorough review to ensure that all transactions are accurately recorded, supported by appropriate documentation, and comply with accounting standards. Obtain necessary approvals from authorized personnel, such as managers or supervisors.

8. **Documentation and Filing:** Maintain proper documentation of the journal entries. Attach or reference the relevant source documents to support each entry. File the journal entries in a systematic manner for future reference, audit purposes, or compliance requirements.

By following these steps, organizations can ensure that journal entries are prepared accurately, reflect the true financial impact of transactions, comply with accounting principles, and provide a reliable foundation for financial reporting and analysis. Taking the time to properly analyze and record transactions helps maintain the integrity and accuracy of the accounting records.

1. **Understand the Transaction:** It is crucial to have a clear understanding of the transaction before journalizing it. Gather all relevant information, such as invoices, receipts, contracts, and other supporting documents, to accurately capture the details of the transaction. Review the documents carefully to ensure that you have a complete understanding of the nature, parties involved, and financial impact of the transaction.

2. **Analyze the Transaction:** Before recording the transaction in a journal entry, it is essential to analyze its impact on the financial accounts. Determine which accounts will be affected and whether they will be debited or credited. Consider the rules of double-entry bookkeeping and the accounting equation to ensure that the journal entry maintains balance and accuracy. This analysis helps in selecting the appropriate accounts and determining the correct debit and credit amounts.

3. **Review Chart of Accounts:** The chart of accounts is a key reference tool in the accounting process. It is a list of all the accounts used in a company's financial system, and each account is assigned a unique code or number. Before performing journal entries, review the chart of accounts to ensure that the accounts you plan to use are correctly identified and categorized. This helps maintain consistency and organization in the accounting records.

4. **Maintain Consistency:** Consistency is crucial in maintaining accurate and reliable accounting records. Before performing journal entries, ensure that you follow consistent naming conventions, formatting, and recording practices. This consistency enables easier tracking, analysis, and reporting of financial transactions over time. Deviating from established practices can lead to confusion and errors in the accounting records.

5. **Check for Accuracy:** Accuracy is paramount in journalizing transactions. Double-check all the figures, account names, and descriptions to ensure they are entered correctly. A small error can have a significant impact on financial statements and analysis. Utilize calculators, software, or other tools to verify calculations and cross-reference information from supporting documents. Accuracy at this stage minimizes the need for adjustments and corrections later on.

6. **Consider Timing and Periods:** Journal entries must be recorded in the appropriate accounting period. Consider the timing of the transaction and ensure that it is accurately reflected in the corresponding period's financial records. Incorrect timing can distort financial statements and misrepresent a company's financial position and performance. Adhering to proper periodization ensures accurate reporting and facilitates financial analysis.

7. **Maintain Supporting Documentation:** Proper recordkeeping extends beyond journal entries. It is essential to maintain supporting documentation for all recorded transactions. This includes invoices, receipts, contracts, bank statements, and any other relevant documents. These documents serve as evidence and support for the journal entries, providing transparency and auditability.

8. **Follow Record Retention Guidelines:** Record retention guidelines outline how long accounting records and supporting documents should be kept.

Before performing journal entries, familiarize yourself with the record retention policies specific to your industry and jurisdiction. Adhering to these guidelines ensures compliance with legal and regulatory requirements and facilitates efficient document management.

By considering these key factors before performing journal entries, businesses can enhance the accuracy, reliability, and efficiency of their recordkeeping processes. Accurate journal entries form the basis for financial reporting, analysis, and decision-making. Taking the time to understand transactions, analyze their impact, review the chart of accounts, maintain consistency, ensure accuracy, consider timing, and adhere to record retention guidelines sets the stage for effective and transparent financial recordkeeping

After Performing Journal Entries

Performing journal entries is a fundamental task in the accounting process, allowing businesses to record and track financial transactions accurately. However, the work does not end once the entries are made. After performing journal entries, there are several important activities that need to be carried out to ensure the completeness, accuracy, and reliability of the accounting records. In this book, we will explore the significance of post-entry activities in accounting and the key steps involved.

After performing journal entries, there are several steps to be taken to ensure the accuracy and completeness of the accounting records. These steps include:

1. **Posting to the General Ledger:** Once the journal entries are prepared, the next step is to post them to the general ledger. Posting involves transferring the information from the journal entries to the respective accounts in the general ledger. Each transaction is posted by debiting or crediting the appropriate accounts, ensuring that the account balances are updated.

2. **Trial Balance:** After posting the journal entries to the general ledger, a trial balance is prepared. The trial balance is a summary of all the account balances, both debit and credit, extracted from the general ledger. It helps to verify the accuracy of the posting process by ensuring that the total debits equal the total credits.

3. **Adjusting Entries**: Adjusting entries may be required to account for certain transactions or events that have not been captured in the regular journal entries. These entries are made at the end of an accounting period to ensure that the financial statements reflect the proper recognition of revenues, expenses, assets, and liabilities. Examples of adjusting entries include accruals, deferrals, depreciation, and allowance for doubtful accounts.

4. **Financial Statements:** Once all the journal entries and adjusting entries are posted, the financial statements can be prepared. The financial statements include the income statement, balance sheet, statement of cash flows, and statement of changes in equity. These statements provide a snapshot of the organization's financial performance, position, cash flows, and changes in equity.

5. **Analysis and Interpretation:** After the financial statements are prepared, they can be analyzed and interpreted to gain insights into the organization's financial health, performance, and trends. Financial ratios, comparisons with industry benchmarks, and other analytical tools can be used to assess the financial condition and make informed decisions.

6. **Closing Entries:** At the end of an accounting period, closing entries are made to transfer the temporary accounts' balances to the retained earnings or owner's equity account. Closing entries reset the temporary accounts (revenues, expenses, and dividends) to zero, preparing them for the next accounting period.

7. **Record Retention:** It is important to retain the documentation of journal entries and supporting documents for a designated period. Proper record retention helps in compliance with legal and regulatory requirements, facilitates audits, and provides a historical record for reference.

8. **Reconciliation:** Reconcile the various accounts and statements to ensure their accuracy and consistency.

This includes reconciling bank statements with the general ledger, accounts receivable and accounts payable with subsidiary records, and any other relevant reconciliations.

9. **Archiving and Retaining Records:** Proper recordkeeping and retention are crucial in accounting. After performing journal entries and completing post-entry activities, it is important to archive and retain all the relevant records and supporting documentation. This includes copies of journal entries, general ledger, trial balance, financial statements, bank statements, invoices, and receipts. Archiving and retaining records serve as evidence, support audits, and ensure compliance with legal and regulatory requirements.

10. **Continual Monitoring and Adjustment:** Accounting is an ongoing process, and post-entry activities involve continual monitoring and adjustment. This includes monitoring the accounts, reviewing financial statements regularly, and making necessary adjustments based on changing circumstances or new information. Continual monitoring ensures the accuracy and relevance of the accounting records and enables proactive decision-making.

By following these steps, organizations can ensure that the journal entries are properly integrated into the general ledger, financial statements are accurate and reliable, and the accounting records are in compliance with accounting principles and standards. These post-journal entry steps contribute to the overall integrity and usefulness of the financial information for decision-making, reporting, and analysis.

Post-entry activities are crucial in accounting to ensure the completeness, accuracy, and reliability of the accounting records. Balancing and verifying accounts, preparing trial balances, making adjusting entries, reviewing financial statements, conducting financial analysis, reconciling accounts, archiving records, and continually monitoring and adjusting are essential steps in the post-entry phase. These activities contribute to the integrity of financial reporting, facilitate informed decision-making, and help businesses maintain compliance with accounting standards and regulations. By giving due attention to post-entry activities, organizations can enhance their financial management and ensure the accuracy and usefulness of their accounting information.

After Performing General Ledger Activities

Performing general ledger activities is a critical step in the accounting process, as it involves updating and maintaining the central repository of financial transactions and account balances. However, the work does not end once the general ledger activities are completed. After performing these activities, there are several important tasks and considerations to address to ensure the accuracy, integrity, and usefulness of financial reporting.

After performing general ledger activities, there are several important steps to take to ensure the accuracy and completeness of the accounting process. These steps include:

1. **Trial Balance:** Prepare a trial balance to verify the accuracy of the general ledger. The trial balance is a summary of all the accounts and their balances extracted from the general ledger. It ensures that the total debits equal the total credits and serves as a preliminary check before preparing financial statements.

2. **Financial Statements:** Use the balances from the general ledger to prepare financial statements. The key financial statements include the income statement, balance sheet, statement of cash flows, and statement of changes in equity. These statements provide a snapshot of the organization's financial performance, position, cash flows, and changes in equity.

3. **Analysis and Interpretation:** Analyze the financial statements to gain insights into the organization's financial health and performance. This involves calculating financial ratios, comparing results with previous periods or industry benchmarks, and conducting trend analysis. These analytical tools help identify strengths, weaknesses, and areas for improvement.

4. **Closing Entries:** At the end of an accounting period, make closing entries to reset temporary accounts and prepare them for the next period. This involves transferring the balances of revenue and expense accounts to the income summary account and then to the retained earnings or owner's equity account.

Closing entries ensure that the revenue and expense accounts start with zero balances in the new period.

5. **Adjusting Entries:** Review the need for adjusting entries to ensure that the financial statements reflect the correct financial position. Adjusting entries are made for items such as accrued revenue or expenses, prepaid expenses, depreciation, and allowance for doubtful accounts. These entries ensure that revenues and expenses are recognized in the appropriate period and that assets and liabilities are properly valued.

6. **Internal Controls and Review:** Implement internal controls to safeguard the accuracy and integrity of the accounting process. This includes segregating duties, reconciling accounts, conducting periodic reviews, and ensuring compliance with relevant regulations and accounting standards. Internal controls help prevent errors, fraud, and misstatements.

7. **Record Retention:** Maintain proper record retention practices to ensure compliance with legal and regulatory requirements. Store and organize financial records, including the general ledger, supporting documents, and financial statements, for the specified period. This facilitates audits, inquiries, and reference purposes.

8. **Financial Analysis and Decision-Making:** Utilize the information from the general ledger and financial statements to make informed decisions. Analyze

financial ratios, trends, and key performance indicators to assess the organization's financial health, identify areas for improvement, and support strategic planning.

9. **Continuous Improvement:** Reflect on the general ledger activities and the overall accounting process to identify areas for improvement. Streamline procedures, enhance controls, and address any issues or discrepancies identified during the process. Continuous improvement ensures the efficiency and effectiveness of the accounting function.

By following these steps, organizations can ensure the accuracy of financial records, produce reliable financial statements, comply with accounting standards, and use financial information to support decision-making and strategic planning. The post-general ledger activities contribute to the overall integrity and usefulness of the accounting information for internal and external stakeholders. In this book, we will explore the significance of post-general ledger activities and the key steps involved.

1. **Reconciliation:** Reconciliation is a crucial post-general ledger activity that involves comparing and matching the balances in the general ledger with external sources of information. This includes reconciling bank statements, accounts receivable, accounts payable, inventory, and other accounts. Reconciliation helps identify discrepancies, errors, or omissions and ensures that the general ledger balances are consistent with the external sources.

Timely reconciliation enhances the accuracy and reliability of financial statements.

2. **Financial Statement Preparation:** After completing general ledger activities, the next step is to prepare financial statements. Financial statements, including the balance sheet, income statement, and statement of cash flows, provide a summary of the company's financial position, results of operations, and cash flows. The financial statement preparation process involves organizing and presenting the financial data in a clear and understandable format, adhering to the applicable accounting standards and reporting guidelines.

3. **Review and Analysis:** Once the financial statements are prepared, they need to be reviewed and analyzed. This involves carefully examining the statements for accuracy, consistency, and adherence to accounting principles. The review process helps identify any potential errors, omissions, or inconsistencies that need to be addressed before finalizing the financial statements. Financial analysis is also conducted to assess the company's financial performance, liquidity, profitability, and overall financial health.

4. **Internal Controls and Compliance:** Post-general ledger activities also involve ensuring the effectiveness of internal controls and compliance with relevant regulations and accounting standards. Internal controls are procedures and measures put in place to safeguard assets, prevent fraud, and ensure the accuracy and reliability of financial reporting. It

is important to review and assess the adequacy of internal controls and take corrective actions if any weaknesses or deficiencies are identified. Compliance with regulatory requirements and accounting standards helps maintain transparency and trust in financial reporting.

5. **Auditing and Assurance:** The completion of general ledger activities sets the stage for auditing and assurance procedures. External auditors or internal audit teams may review the general ledger, financial statements, and supporting documentation to provide independent assurance regarding the fairness, accuracy, and completeness of the financial information. Cooperation and collaboration with auditors during the auditing process are crucial to address any issues or questions that may arise.

6. **Archiving and Retaining Records:** Proper recordkeeping and retention are essential after performing general ledger activities. It is important to archive and retain all the relevant records and supporting documentation, including general ledger reports, financial statements, reconciliations, and audit trails. Archiving and retaining records serve as evidence, support audits, facilitate future analysis, and ensure compliance with legal and regulatory requirements.

7. **Continuous Monitoring and Improvement:** General ledger activities should be part of an ongoing process of continuous monitoring and improvement. Regular monitoring of account balances,

transactional activity, and financial statements helps detect and correct errors, identify trends or anomalies, and ensure the accuracy and integrity of financial reporting. Continuous improvement involves identifying areas for process enhancement, automation opportunities, and implementing best practices to streamline general ledger activities and enhance efficiency.

Post-general ledger activities play a crucial role in ensuring the accuracy, integrity, and usefulness of financial reporting. Reconciliation, financial statement preparation, review and analysis, internal controls and compliance, auditing and assurance, archiving records, and continuous monitoring are key steps to address after performing general ledger activities. These activities contribute to the reliability and transparency of financial information, support informed decision-making, and help organizations meet their reporting obligations. By giving due attention to post-general ledger activities, businesses can maintain the integrity of their financial records and promote trust among stakeholders

The Normal Balance of Asset and Expense Accounts

In financial accounting, **all asset and expense accounts have debit balances**. This accounting principle is based on the fundamental concept of double-entry bookkeeping, where every transaction has equal debits and credits to maintain the balance in the accounting equation. To understand why asset and expense accounts have debit balances, it's important to grasp the basic structure of a balance sheet and the nature of these accounts.

Assets are resources owned by a company that have economic value. They include cash, accounts receivable, inventory, property, plant, and equipment, among others. When an asset account is increased, it is debited to reflect the inflow or acquisition of an asset. For example, when a company receives cash from a customer, the cash account is debited to increase the cash balance.

Expenses, on the other hand, represent the costs incurred in the process of generating revenue. They include items such as salaries, utilities, rent, and supplies. When an expense is incurred, it is debited to recognize the decrease in assets or the increase in liabilities. For instance, when a company pays its monthly rent, the rent expense account is debited to reflect the decrease in cash or increase in accounts payable.

The reason asset and expense accounts have debit balances lies in the traditional accounting system's rules and conventions. According to this system, debits are used to record increases in asset accounts and expenses. Conversely, credits are used to record decreases in asset accounts and expenses, as well as increases in liability, equity, and revenue accounts.

By adhering to this system, companies can maintain accurate financial records and ensure that the accounting equation remains in balance. The accounting equation states that assets equal liabilities plus equity, and it forms the foundation of double-entry bookkeeping. When a transaction occurs, the debit entry is recorded on the left side of the account, while the credit entry is recorded on the right side. This process maintains the equilibrium of debits and credits in the accounting system. Consequently, asset and expense accounts will typically have debit balances since they receive more debits than credits.

It's essential to note that not all accounts have debit balances. Liability, equity, and revenue accounts typically have credit balances. Liability accounts represent the company's obligations, such as accounts payable and loans payable. Equity accounts show the ownership interest in the company, including retained earnings and capital. Revenue accounts record the income generated by the company's core operations.

All asset and expense accounts have debit balances in financial accounting. This convention is based on the principles of double-entry bookkeeping and ensures that the accounting equation remains in balance. Debits are used to record increases in assets and expenses, while credits are used for decreases in assets and expenses, as well as increases in liability, equity, and revenue accounts. By understanding these principles and maintaining accurate records, companies can effectively track their financial activities and make informed business decisions.

Increase and Decrease to the Asset and Expense Accounts – Debit

When we say that all asset and expense accounts balances are on the debit side, we are referring to the normal balance of these accounts in the double-entry bookkeeping system. In this system, every transaction has two sides: a debit and a credit. The debit side represents the increase or decrease in assets, while the credit side represents the increase or decrease in liabilities, equity, and revenue. In accounting, the fundamental accounting equation is Assets = Liabilities + Equity. This equation must always remain in balance, which means that the total debits must equal the total credits. To maintain this balance, certain types of accounts have normal debit or credit balances.

Asset accounts, such as cash, accounts receivable, inventory, and property, plant, and equipment, are considered to have a normal debit balance. This means that increases to these accounts are recorded as debits, while decreases are recorded as credits. For example, when a company receives cash from a customer, it will debit the cash account to increase its balance.

Expense accounts, such as salaries expense, rent expense, and utilities expense, also have normal debit balances. These accounts represent costs or expenses incurred by the company. When expenses are incurred, they are recorded as debits, reducing the company's net income. For example, when a company pays its employees' salaries, it will debit the salaries expense account to recognize the expense.

On the other hand, liability, equity, and revenue accounts have normal credit balances. Liabilities, such as accounts payable and loans payable, represent obligations or debts owed by the company. Increases in liabilities are recorded as credits, while decreases are recorded as debits. Equity accounts, including retained earnings and owner's capital, also have normal credit balances. Increases in equity are recorded as credits, such as when the company generates profits. Revenue accounts, such as sales revenue and service revenue, represent the company's income. Increases in revenue are recorded as credits.

It's important to note that while asset and expense accounts have normal debit balances, this doesn't mean that they can only have debit entries. Depending on the transaction, there may be occasions when these accounts have credit entries. However, in general, the normal balance for these accounts is on the debit side. Understanding the normal balances of different accounts is crucial for recording transactions accurately and preparing financial statements. It helps ensure that the accounting equation remains in balance and provides a systematic way to track the financial position and performance of a company. By following the principles of double-entry bookkeeping and recognizing the normal balances of accounts, accountants can maintain accurate records and generate reliable financial information.

Computations and Balances:

1. Cash Receipts:
   - Computation: Total cash receipts = Cash sales + Collections from accounts receivable
   - Example: A retail store receives $2,000 in cash sales and collects $3,000 from accounts receivable. The total cash receipts would be $2,000 + $3,000 = $5,000.

2. Purchase of Equipment:
   - Computation: Total cost of equipment = Purchase price + Installation costs
   - Example: A company purchases equipment for $10,000 and incurs $1,000 in installation costs. The total cost of the equipment would be $10,000 + $1,000 = $11,000.

3. Repayment of Loan:
   - Computation: Total loan repayment = Principal payment + Interest payment
   - Example: A company repays a loan with a principal payment of $5,000 and an interest payment of $1,000. The total loan repayment would be $5,000 + $1,000 = $6,000.

4. Inventory Cost of Goods Sold:
   - Computation: Cost of goods sold = Beginning inventory + Purchases - Ending inventory
   - Example: A company starts with an inventory of $50,000, makes purchases of $30,000, and ends with an inventory of $40,000. The cost of goods sold would be $50,000 + $30,000 - $40,000 = $40,000.

5. Depreciation Expense:
   - Computation: Depreciation expense = (Asset cost - Salvage value) / Useful life
   - Example: A company purchases a vehicle for $20,000 with an estimated useful life of 5 years and a salvage value of $2,000. The annual depreciation expense would be ($20,000 - $2,000) / 5 = $3,600.

6. Accrued Salaries:
   - Computation: Accrued salaries = Number of days × Daily salary rate
   - Example: An employee's daily salary rate is $100, and they worked for 5 days in the

current pay period. The accrued salaries would be $100 × 5 = $500.

7. Prepaid Insurance Allocation:
   - Computation: Prepaid insurance allocation = Prepaid insurance / Insurance coverage period
   - Example: A company pre-pays $1,200 for a one-year insurance policy. The monthly prepaid insurance allocation would be $1,200 / 12 = $100.

1. Depreciation Expense:
   - Computation: Depreciation expense = (Asset cost - Salvage value) / Useful life
   - Example: A company purchases a machine for $10,000 with an estimated useful life of 5 years and a salvage value of $2,000. The annual depreciation expense would be ($10,000 - $2,000) / 5 = $1,600.

2. Inventory Valuation:
   - Computation: Ending inventory = Beginning inventory + Purchases - Cost of goods sold
   - Example: A retailer starts with an inventory of $50,000, makes purchases of $30,000 during the year, and reports a cost of goods sold of $40,000. The ending inventory would be $50,000 + $30,000 - $40,000 = $40,000.

3. Bad Debt Expense:
   - Computation: Bad debt expense = Sales revenue × Bad debt percentage

- Example: A company has sales revenue of $100,000 and estimates that 5% of the sales will result in bad debts. The bad debt expense would be $100,000 × 0.05 = $5,000.

4. Prepaid Expense Allocation:
   - Computation: Prepaid expense allocation = Prepaid expense / Useful life
   - Example: A company pre-pays $12,000 for a two-year insurance policy. The annual prepaid expense allocation would be $12,000 / 2 = $6,000.

5. Amortization Expense:
   - Computation: Amortization expense = Intangible asset cost / Amortization period
   - Example: A company acquires a patent for $60,000 with a legal life of 10 years. The annual amortization expense would be $60,000 / 10 = $6,000.

6. Research and Development Expense Capitalization:
   - Computation: Research and development expense capitalized = Direct costs + Indirect costs
   - Example: A company incurs $50,000 in direct costs and $20,000 in indirect costs related to a research and development project. The research and development expense capitalized would be $50,000 + $20,000 = $70,000.

7. Operating Lease Expense Recognition:
   - Computation: Operating lease expense = Annual lease payments / Lease term
   - Example: A company signs a five-year lease agreement with annual lease payments of $10,000. The annual operating lease expense would be $10,000.

These computations and examples illustrate how different transactions and events related to asset and expense accounts are calculated and recorded. They demonstrate the application of accounting principles and conventions to ensure accurate financial reporting and decision-making. It is important to consult with accounting standards and guidelines specific to your jurisdiction when performing such computations.

Owner's Equity, Revenue and Liability Accounts

In financial accounting, it is a general principle that all liability, owners' equity, and revenue accounts have credit balances. The concept of credit balances for liability, owners' equity, and revenue accounts can be better understood by examining the nature and purpose of these accounts. This principle is based on the double-entry bookkeeping system, which ensures that every transaction is recorded with equal debits and credits, maintaining the balance in the accounting equation. This convention is based on the principles of double-entry bookkeeping, where credits are used to record increases in these accounts. By maintaining accurate records and balancing the accounting equation, companies can track their financial activities and assess their financial position.

To understand why liability, owners' equity, and revenue accounts have credit balances, it is important to have a basic understanding of their nature and how they contribute to the financial position of a company.

Liability accounts represent the company's obligations to pay debts or fulfill certain responsibilities. They include accounts payable, loans payable, and accrued expenses. When a liability is incurred, it is recorded as a credit to reflect the increase in the company's obligations. For example, when a company receives goods on credit from a supplier, the accounts payable account is credited to reflect the increase in the liability.

Owners' equity accounts represent the ownership interest in the company. They include common stock, retained earnings, and additional paid-in capital. When owners invest capital into the business or when the company generates profits, these accounts are credited to reflect the increase in the owners' equity. For instance, when a company issues additional shares of stock, the common stock account is credited to record the increase in equity.

Revenue accounts represent the income earned by a company through its primary operations. They include sales revenue, service revenue, and interest revenue. When a company generates revenue, it is recorded as a credit to recognize the increase in the company's financial resources. For example, when a company sells products to customers and receives payment, the sales revenue account is credited to reflect the increase in revenue.

The reason liability, owners' equity, and revenue accounts have credit balances is based on the principles of double-entry bookkeeping. In this system, credits are used to record increases in liability and equity accounts, as well as revenue accounts. Conversely, debits are used to record decreases in these accounts, as well as increases in asset and expense accounts.

By following this system, companies can maintain accurate financial records and ensure the balance of the accounting equation. The accounting equation states that assets equal liabilities plus owners' equity. Therefore, for the equation to remain in balance, the credit entries in liability, owners' equity, and revenue accounts need to match the debit entries in asset and expense accounts.

It is important to note that not all accounts have credit balances. Asset and expense accounts typically have debit balances, as they represent the resources owned by the company and the costs incurred in generating revenue. These accounts receive more debit entries than credit entries.

Liability accounts represent the financial obligations or debts owed by a company to external parties. Examples of liability accounts include accounts payable, loans payable, and accrued expenses. When a liability is incurred, such as when a company purchases goods or services on credit, it increases the company's obligations to pay in the future. To record this increase, liability accounts are credited.

Owners' equity accounts, also known as shareholders' equity or stockholders' equity, represent the residual interest in the assets of a company after deducting liabilities. These accounts capture the owners' claims on the company's assets. Owners' equity accounts include common stock, retained earnings, and additional paid-in capital. When owners invest additional capital into the business or when the company generates profits, these accounts are credited to reflect the increase in the owners' equity.

Revenue accounts record the income earned by a company through its primary operations. Examples of revenue accounts include sales revenue, service revenue, and interest revenue. When a company sells products, provides services, or earns interest income, it recognizes revenue by crediting the corresponding revenue accounts. This credit entry reflects the increase in the company's financial resources resulting from the revenue generation.

The reason liability, owners' equity, and revenue accounts have credit balances is based on the underlying principles of the double-entry bookkeeping system. According to this system, every financial transaction has equal and offsetting debits and credits. Debits are used to record increases in asset accounts and expense accounts, while credits are used to record increases in liability, owners' equity, and revenue accounts.

Maintaining credit balances in these accounts ensures that the fundamental accounting equation remains in balance. The accounting equation states that assets equal liabilities plus owners' equity. By crediting liability and owners' equity accounts for increases and crediting revenue accounts for income, the equation is maintained.

The use of credit balances in liability, owners' equity, and revenue accounts facilitates financial analysis and reporting. It provides a clear picture of the company's financial obligations, the owners' claims on the company's assets, and the revenue generated from business operations. These credit balances are critical in determining the financial position, profitability, and performance of a company.

Understanding the nature of credit balances in liability, owners' equity, and revenue accounts is crucial for financial professionals, including accountants, auditors, and financial analysts. By accurately recording and analyzing transactions, they can ensure the integrity of financial statements and provide valuable insights for decision-making.

All liability, owners' equity, and revenue accounts have credit balances in financial accounting. This principle is based on the double-entry bookkeeping system, where credits are used to record increases in these accounts. By adhering to this principle, companies can maintain accurate financial records, fulfill their obligations, track owners' claims on assets, and report revenue generated from business operations.

Computations and Examples:

1. Computation: Recording a liability for accounts payable. Example: ABC Company purchases inventory on credit for $1,000. The journal entry would be: Accounts Payable (Liability) $1,000 Inventory (Asset) $1,000

2. Computation: Recognizing revenue from the sale of goods. Example: XYZ Company sells products for $5,000 in cash. The journal entry would be: Cash (Asset) $5,000 Sales Revenue (Revenue) $5,000

3. Computation: Issuing common stock for capital. Example: DEF Company issues 1,000 shares of common stock for $10 per share. The journal entry would be: Cash (Asset) $10,000 Common Stock (Owners' Equity) $10,000

4. Computation: Recording a liability for a bank loan. Example: GHI Company obtains a bank loan of $50,000. The journal entry would be: Cash (Asset) $50,000 Bank Loan (Liability) $50,000

5. Computation: Recognizing revenue from services rendered. Example: JKL Company provides consulting services for $2,500 on credit. The journal entry would be: Accounts Receivable (Asset) $2,500 Service Revenue (Revenue) $2,500

6. Computation: Declaring dividends to shareholders. Example: MNO Company declares a dividend of $1 per share on 1,000 shares of common stock. The journal entry would be: Dividends Payable (Liability) $1,000 Retained Earnings (Owners' Equity) $1,000

7. Computation: Recognizing revenue from rental income. Example: PQR Company receives $1,200 in

rent for a property. The journal entry would be: Cash (Asset) $1,200 Rental Income (Revenue) $1,200

8. Computation: Recording a liability for accrued expenses. Example: STU Company accrues $500 for unpaid salaries. The journal entry would be: Salaries Expense (Expense) $500 Salaries Payable (Liability) $500

9. Computation: Recognizing revenue from interest income. Example: VWX Company earns $500 in interest from a bond investment. The journal entry would be: Cash (Asset) $500 Interest Income (Revenue) $500

10. Computation: Recording an increase in owners' equity from net income. Example: YZA Company generates $10,000 in net income. The journal entry would be: Retained Earnings (Owners' Equity) $10,000 Net Income (Revenue) $10,000

These computations and examples illustrate how liability, owners' equity, and revenue accounts are credited to reflect increases in financial obligations, capital contributions, and income generated by a business. By understanding and applying these principles, financial professionals can accurately record transactions and maintain the balance and integrity of the company's financial statements.

Asset Sub-Accounts Increase

The asset sub-accounts increase when there are transactions that result in the acquisition or addition of assets to the organization. The specific point at which the asset sub-accounts increase depends on the nature of the transaction and the accounting policies of the organization. Here are some common scenarios when the asset sub-accounts increase:

1. **Purchasing Assets:** When an organization purchases assets, such as property, equipment, or vehicles, the asset sub-accounts related to those specific assets increase. This increase occurs when the assets are recorded in the accounting records at their cost or fair value.

2. **Capital Expenditures:** Capital expenditures involve spending on assets that provide long-term benefits to the organization. For example, investing in the construction of a new building or the development of software. The asset sub-accounts increase when these expenditures are capitalized, meaning they are recorded as assets rather than expenses.

3. **Depreciation and Amortization:** Depreciation and amortization represent the allocation of the cost of long-term assets over their useful lives. Each accounting period, a portion of the asset's value is recorded as an expense, and the corresponding asset sub-account decreases. However, the overall value of the asset remains the same.

4. **Revaluation of Assets:** In some cases, assets may be revalued to reflect their fair value or current market value. This usually occurs when there are significant changes in market conditions or the value of the asset has materially changed. When assets are revalued

upwards, the asset sub-accounts increase to reflect the new higher value.

5. **Contributions and Donations:** Nonprofit organizations may receive contributions or donations in the form of assets. These assets are recorded as increases in the corresponding asset sub-accounts. For example, if a nonprofit organization receives a donation of land, the land asset sub-account will increase to reflect the addition of the donated asset.

6. **Internal Transfers:** In some cases, assets may be transferred internally within an organization. For instance, if one department transfers equipment to another department, the asset sub-accounts for both departments are adjusted to reflect the change in ownership or location of the asset.

It's important to note that the specific accounts and sub-accounts used to track assets can vary depending on the organization's chart of accounts and accounting policies. The increase in asset sub-accounts occurs as a result of the appropriate recording and recognition of the asset transactions in accordance with generally accepted accounting principles (GAAP) or other applicable accounting standards.

Asset Sub-Accounts Decrease

The asset sub-accounts decrease when there are transactions or events that result in a reduction or disposal of assets from the organization. The specific point at which the asset sub-accounts decrease depends on the nature of the transaction and the accounting policies of the organization. Here are some common scenarios when the asset sub-accounts decrease:

1. **Sale or Disposal of Assets:** When an organization sells or disposes of an asset, the corresponding asset sub-account decreases. This decrease occurs when the organization recognizes the loss of control or ownership over the asset and removes it from the accounting records. The decrease is typically recorded at the proceeds received from the sale or the fair value of the asset at the time of disposal.

2. **Depreciation and Amortization:** As mentioned earlier, depreciation and amortization represent the allocation of the cost of long-term assets over their useful lives. Each accounting period, a portion of the asset's value is recorded as an expense, and the corresponding asset sub-account decreases. This reflects the reduction in the value of the asset due to its consumption or obsolescence.

3. **Impairment:** If the value of an asset is impaired, meaning its carrying value exceeds its recoverable amount, the asset sub-account is decreased to reflect the impairment loss. This occurs when there is a significant and permanent decrease in the future economic benefits expected from the asset. The impairment loss is recognized as an expense, and the asset is written down to its recoverable amount.

4. **Retirement or Decommissioning:** When an asset reaches the end of its useful life or is no longer in

service, it is retired or decommissioned. The corresponding asset sub-account decreases as the organization recognizes the removal of the asset from its books. Retirement or decommissioning can occur for assets such as machinery, equipment, or vehicles that are no longer functional or productive.

5. **Exchanges or Transfers:** If an asset is exchanged for another asset or transferred to a different entity or department within the organization, the asset sub-account for the original asset decreases. This reduction reflects the change in ownership or location of the asset.

6. **Revaluation or Write-Down:** In some cases, assets may be revalued downwards to reflect a decrease in their fair value or current market value. This occurs when there is a significant decline in the asset's value. The asset sub-account is decreased to reflect the new lower value.

It's important to note that the specific accounts and sub-accounts used to track assets can vary depending on the organization's chart of accounts and accounting policies. The decrease in asset sub-accounts occurs as a result of the appropriate recording and recognition of the asset transactions or events in accordance with generally accepted accounting principles (GAAP) or other applicable accounting standards.

Liability Sub-Accounts Increase

The liability sub-accounts increase when there are transactions or events that result in the creation or increase of obligations or debts for the organization. The specific point at which the liability sub-accounts increase depends on the nature of the transaction and the accounting policies of the organization. Here are some common scenarios when the liability sub-accounts increase:

1. **Borrowing Funds:** When an organization borrows funds from external sources such as banks, financial institutions, or bondholders, the liability sub-accounts increase. This increase occurs when the organization receives the funds and recognizes the corresponding debt obligation in its accounting records. The liability sub-accounts capture the amount borrowed, including any interest or fees associated with the borrowing.

2. **Accounts Payable:** When an organization purchases goods or services on credit from suppliers or vendors, an accounts payable liability is created. The liability sub-account increases to reflect the amount owed to the suppliers or vendors. This increase occurs at the time of the purchase or receipt of the goods or services, and it represents the organization's obligation to make payment in the future.

3. **Accrued Expenses:** Accrued expenses represent expenses that have been incurred but not yet paid. Examples include salaries and wages, utility bills, or interest expenses. The liability sub-accounts increase

to recognize these accrued expenses. This increase occurs at the end of the accounting period when the expenses have been incurred but not yet paid, and it reflects the organization's obligation to settle these expenses in the future.

4. **Unearned Revenue:** Unearned revenue represents advance payments or receipts from customers for goods or services that have not yet been delivered or earned. The liability sub-accounts increase to record the unearned revenue. This increase occurs at the time the payment or receipt is received, and it represents the organization's obligation to deliver the goods or services in the future.

5. **Contingent Liabilities:** Contingent liabilities are potential obligations that may arise in the future depending on the outcome of uncertain events, such as pending lawsuits or potential warranty claims. When a contingent liability is probable and its amount can be reasonably estimated, the liability sub-accounts increase to reflect the potential obligation. This increase occurs when the contingency is recognized and disclosed in the financial statements.

6. **Deferred Income Taxes:** Deferred income taxes arise when there are temporary differences between the timing of recognizing income or expenses for tax purposes and financial reporting purposes. The liability sub-accounts increase to record the deferred income taxes. This increase occurs when the temporary differences arise, and it represents the

organization's obligation to pay taxes on the deferred amounts in future periods.

It's important to note that the specific accounts and sub-accounts used to track liabilities can vary depending on the organization's chart of accounts and accounting policies. The increase in liability sub-accounts occurs as a result of the appropriate recording and recognition of the liability transactions or events in accordance with generally accepted accounting principles (GAAP) or other applicable accounting standards.

Liability Sub-Accounts Decrease

The liability sub-accounts decrease when there are transactions or events that result in the reduction or settlement of obligations or debts of the organization. The specific point at which the liability sub-accounts decrease depends on the nature of the transaction and the accounting policies of the organization. Here are some common scenarios when the liability sub-accounts decrease:

1. **Repayment of Borrowed Funds:** When an organization repays borrowed funds to lenders or creditors, the liability sub-accounts decrease. This decrease occurs when the organization makes payments towards the principal amount of the debt, reducing the outstanding balance. The decrease in the liability sub-account reflects the reduction in the organization's debt obligation.

2. **Settlement of Accounts Payable:** When an organization pays its suppliers or vendors for goods

or services previously purchased on credit, the accounts payable liability is reduced. The liability sub-account decreases to reflect the payment made, indicating that the organization has fulfilled its obligation to the suppliers or vendors.

3. **Expense Accrual Reversal:** If an expense has been accrued but is subsequently determined to be no longer applicable or has been overestimated, the liability sub-account for the accrued expense is decreased. This decrease occurs when the organization reverses the accrual, removing the previously recognized obligation from the accounting records.

4. **Revenue Recognition:** In certain cases, when unearned revenue is earned, the liability sub-accounts decrease. This occurs when the organization delivers goods or services to customers, fulfilling its obligation and converting the previously recognized unearned revenue into revenue. The decrease in the liability sub-account is accompanied by an increase in the corresponding revenue account.

5. **Settlement of Contingent Liabilities:** If a contingent liability is resolved and the organization becomes legally released from the potential obligation, the liability sub-account for the contingent liability is decreased. This decrease occurs when the contingent liability is settled, and the organization's obligation is extinguished.

6. **Tax Payments:** When an organization makes tax payments to tax authorities, the liability sub-accounts related to tax liabilities decrease. This decrease occurs when the organization settles its tax obligations, reducing the outstanding liability. The decrease in the liability sub-account reflects the reduction in the organization's tax obligation.

It's important to note that the specific accounts and sub-accounts used to track liabilities can vary depending on the organization's chart of accounts and accounting policies. The decrease in liability sub-accounts occurs as a result of the appropriate recording and recognition of the liability transactions or events in accordance with generally accepted accounting principles (GAAP) or other applicable accounting standards.

Owners' Equity Sub-Accounts Increase

The owners' equity sub-accounts increase when there are transactions or events that result in the accumulation or addition of value to the owners' equity of the organization. The specific point at which the owners' equity sub-accounts increase depends on the nature of the transaction and the accounting policies of the organization. Here are some common scenarios when the owners' equity sub-accounts increase:

1. **Investments by Owners:** When owners contribute additional capital to the organization, the owners' equity sub-accounts increase. This increase occurs when the organization receives the additional capital and recognizes it as an increase in the owners' equity.

It reflects the owners' increased investment in the business.

2. **Retained Earnings:** Retained earnings represent the accumulated profits or earnings that have been retained in the business after dividends or distributions to owners. When the organization generates profits or net income, the retained earnings sub-account increases. This increase occurs at the end of the accounting period when the organization closes its income and expense accounts, transferring the net income to the retained earnings sub-account.

3. **Revaluation of Assets:** In some cases, assets may be revalued upwards to reflect their fair value or current market value. This revaluation can result in an increase in the owners' equity sub-accounts. It occurs when there is a significant increase in the value of the asset, and the organization recognizes the gain in its financial statements.

4. **Comprehensive Income:** Comprehensive income includes all changes in equity during a period, except those resulting from investments by owners and distributions to owners. It includes items such as gains or losses from foreign currency translations, unrealized gains or losses on investments, and changes in the fair value of certain financial instruments. When these items are recognized in the financial statements, the owners' equity sub-accounts increase to reflect the comprehensive income.

5. **Profit from Operations:** If the organization generates profits or income from its regular business operations, the owners' equity sub-accounts increase. This occurs when revenues exceed expenses, resulting in net income. The net income is added to the owners' equity through the retained earnings sub-account or directly to specific equity accounts, depending on the organization's accounting policies.

6. **Additional Paid-in Capital:** Additional paid-in capital represents the amount received from issuing shares of stock above their par or stated value. When the organization issues share at a price higher than their par or stated value, the additional paid-in capital sub-account increases. This increase reflects the additional value contributed by shareholders above the nominal value of the shares.

It's important to note that the specific accounts and sub-accounts used to track owners' equity can vary depending on the organization's chart of accounts and accounting policies. The increase in owners' equity sub-accounts occurs as a result of the appropriate recording and recognition of the equity transactions or events in accordance with generally accepted accounting principles (GAAP) or other applicable accounting standards.

The Owners' Equity Sub-Accounts Decrease

The owners' equity sub-accounts decrease when there are transactions or events that result in the reduction or distribution of value from the owners' equity of the organization. The specific point at which the owners' equity sub-accounts decrease depends on the nature of the transaction and the accounting policies of the organization. Here are some common scenarios when the owners' equity sub-accounts decrease:

1. **Dividends or Distributions:** When the organization distributes profits or earnings to owners, the owners' equity sub-accounts decrease. This decrease occurs when dividends or distributions are declared and paid to the owners. It reflects the reduction in the retained earnings or specific equity accounts attributable to the owners.

2. **Share Buybacks or Repurchases:** If the organization repurchases its own shares from shareholders, the owners' equity sub-accounts decrease. This decrease occurs when the shares are retired or held as treasury stock, reducing the number of outstanding shares and decreasing the shareholders' equity. The amount used to repurchase the shares is deducted from the owners' equity.

3. **Losses from Operations:** If the organization incurs losses or expenses that exceed revenues or income, the owners' equity sub-accounts decrease. This occurs when the organization recognizes a net loss, which reduces the retained earnings or specific equity accounts. Losses from operations are subtracted from the owners' equity, reflecting the reduction in value.

4. **Revaluation or Write-Down of Assets:** In some cases, assets may be revalued downwards to reflect a

decrease in their fair value or current market value. This can result in a decrease in the owners' equity sub-accounts. It occurs when there is a significant decrease in the value of the asset, and the organization recognizes the loss in its financial statements.

5. **Liquidation or Dissolution:** In the event of the liquidation or dissolution of the organization, the owners' equity sub-accounts decrease as the assets are distributed to the owners or used to settle liabilities. This process involves the reduction or elimination of the owners' equity accounts as the organization ceases its operations.

It's important to note that the specific accounts and sub-accounts used to track owners' equity can vary depending on the organization's chart of accounts and accounting policies. The decrease in owners' equity sub-accounts occurs as a result of the appropriate recording and recognition of the equity transactions or events in accordance with generally accepted accounting principles (GAAP) or other applicable accounting standards.

Revenue Sub-Accounts Increase

The revenue sub-accounts increase when there are transactions or events that result in the generation or recognition of revenue for the organization. The specific point at which the revenue sub-accounts increase depends on the nature of the transaction and the accounting policies of the organization. Here are some common scenarios when the revenue sub-accounts increase:

1. **Sale of Goods:** When an organization sells goods to customers, the revenue sub-accounts increase. This increase occurs at the point of sale when the organization transfers control of the goods to the customer and has the right to receive payment. The revenue recognized represents the amount earned from the sale of goods.

2. **Rendering of Services:** If the organization provides services to customers, the revenue sub-accounts increase. This increase occurs when the services are performed, and the organization has the right to receive payment. The revenue recognized represents the value of the services provided.

3. **Rental Income:** If the organization earns rental income from leasing or renting out assets such as property or equipment, the revenue sub-accounts increase. This increase occurs when the rental period begins, and the organization is entitled to receive the rental payments. The revenue recognized represents the rental income earned.

4. **Interest Income:** When the organization earns interest on loans, investments, or other interest-bearing assets, the revenue sub-accounts increase. This increase occurs over time as interest is earned or at specific intervals depending on the terms of the interest-bearing arrangement. The revenue recognized represents the interest income earned.

5. **Licensing or Royalty Fees:** If the organization receives licensing fees or royalties for the use of its

intellectual property, patents, copyrights, or trademarks, the revenue sub-accounts increase. This increase occurs when the licensing agreement or royalty arrangement is in effect, and the organization is entitled to receive the fees or royalties. The revenue recognized represents the licensing or royalty income earned.

6. **Commissions or Fees:** If the organization earns commissions or fees for acting as an intermediary or providing specific services, the revenue sub-accounts increase. This increase occurs when the organization completes the required activities or fulfills its obligations, and it becomes entitled to receive the commissions or fees. The revenue recognized represents the commissions or fees earned.

It's important to note that the specific accounts and sub-accounts used to track revenue can vary depending on the organization's chart of accounts and accounting policies. The increase in revenue sub-accounts occurs as a result of the appropriate recording and recognition of the revenue transactions or events in accordance with generally accepted accounting principles (GAAP) or other applicable accounting standards.

Revenue Sub-Accounts Decrease

The revenue sub-accounts decrease when there are transactions or events that result in the reversal, adjustment, or reduction of previously recognized revenue. The specific point at which the revenue sub-accounts decrease depends on the nature of the transaction and the accounting policies of the organization. Here are some common scenarios when the revenue sub-accounts decrease:

1. **Sales Returns and Allowances:** If customers return goods or receive allowances for damaged or defective goods, the revenue sub-accounts decrease. This decrease occurs when the organization grants the return or allowance and recognizes a reduction in the revenue previously recorded for the sale. The amount of the return or allowance is subtracted from the revenue sub-account.

2. **Sales Discounts:** If the organization offers discounts to customers for early payment or other reasons, the revenue sub-accounts decrease. This decrease occurs when the discount is granted and recognized as a reduction in the revenue previously recorded for the sale. The amount of the discount is subtracted from the revenue sub-account.

3. **Contract Modifications or Changes:** If there are modifications or changes to long-term contracts, such as changes in scope, pricing, or terms, the revenue sub-accounts may decrease. This decrease occurs when the organization reassesses the contract and recognizes a reduction in the revenue previously recognized based on the revised terms or estimates. The decrease reflects the adjustment to the revenue recognized.

4. **Provision for Uncollectible Accounts:** If the organization estimates that it will not be able to collect the full number of accounts receivable, a provision for uncollectible accounts is recognized. This provision reduces the revenue sub-account, reflecting the expected losses from uncollectible amounts.

5. **Contract Losses:** If the organization determines that it will not be able to recover the costs incurred on a contract or project, a loss is recognized. This loss reduces the revenue sub-account and is recorded to reflect the shortfall between the costs incurred and the expected revenue from the contract.

6. **Adjustments or Corrections:** In some cases, errors or adjustments may be identified that require the correction of previously recognized revenue. This can happen due to accounting errors, changes in accounting estimates, or the discovery of fraud or misstatement. The revenue sub-accounts decrease to correct the previously overstated revenue or to adjust for the error or misstatement.

It's important to note that the specific accounts and sub-accounts used to track revenue can vary depending on the organization's chart of accounts and accounting policies. The decrease in revenue sub-accounts occurs as a result of the appropriate recording and recognition of the revenue adjustments or events in accordance with generally accepted accounting principles (GAAP) or other applicable accounting standards.

Expense Sub-Accounts Increase

The expense sub-accounts increase when there are transactions or events that result in the incurrence or recognition of expenses by the organization. The specific point at which the expense sub-accounts increase depends on the nature of the transaction and the accounting policies of the organization. Here are some common scenarios when the expense sub-accounts increase:

1. **Purchase of Goods or Services:** When the organization purchases goods or services for its operations, the expense sub-accounts increase. This increase occurs at the point of purchase or receipt of the goods or services, and it reflects the cost incurred by the organization. Examples include the purchase of inventory, raw materials, office supplies, or hiring external services.

2. **Employee Salaries and Benefits:** If the organization pays salaries, wages, or benefits to its employees, the expense sub-accounts increase. This increase occurs when the organization incurs the cost of compensating its employees for their services. Examples include regular payroll expenses, employee benefits such as healthcare or retirement contributions, and payroll taxes.

3. **Rent and Utilities:** When the organization pays rent for its premises or utilities such as electricity, water, or internet services, the expense sub-accounts increase. This increase occurs as the organization

incurs the costs associated with occupying and operating its physical facilities.

4. **Advertising and Marketing:** If the organization engages in advertising or marketing activities to promote its products or services, the expense sub-accounts increase. This increase occurs when the organization incurs costs for advertising campaigns, marketing materials, online advertisements, or other promotional activities.

5. **Depreciation and Amortization:** When the organization allocates the cost of its long-term assets over their useful lives, the expense sub-accounts increase. This increase occurs as the organization recognizes the periodic depreciation or amortization expense associated with its property, plant, and equipment or intangible assets.

6. **Professional Fees:** If the organization engages external professionals such as consultants, lawyers, or accountants, the expense sub-accounts increase. This increase occurs when the organization incurs costs for professional services rendered.

7. **Repairs and Maintenance:** When the organization incurs expenses for the repair, maintenance, or servicing of its assets or equipment, the expense sub-accounts increase. This increase reflects the costs associated with keeping the assets in working order and maintaining their functionality.

It's important to note that the specific accounts and sub-accounts used to track expenses can vary depending on the organization's chart of accounts and accounting policies. The increase in expense sub-accounts occurs as a result of the appropriate recording and recognition of the expense transactions or events in accordance with generally accepted accounting principles (GAAP) or other applicable accounting standards.

The Expense Sub-Accounts Decrease

The expense sub-accounts decrease when there are transactions or events that result in the reversal, adjustment, or reduction of previously recognized expenses. The specific point at which the expense sub-accounts decrease depends on the nature of the transaction and the accounting policies of the organization. Here are some common scenarios when the expense sub-accounts decrease:

1. **Returns or Allowances:** If the organization returns goods to suppliers or receives allowances for damaged or defective goods, the expense sub-accounts decrease. This decrease occurs when the organization records the return or allowance and recognizes a reduction in the previously recognized expense for the purchase. The amount of the return or allowance is subtracted from the expense sub-account.

2. **Adjustments or Corrections:** In some cases, errors or adjustments may be identified that require the correction of previously recognized expenses. This can happen due to accounting errors, changes in

accounting estimates, or the discovery of fraud or misstatement. The expense sub-accounts decrease to correct the previously overstated expenses or to adjust for the error or misstatement.

3. **Reversal of Accruals:** If the organization previously recognized accruals for expenses that are no longer applicable, the expense sub-accounts decrease. This can happen when the organization estimated and recorded expenses for which the obligation is no longer required or when there was an overestimate of the amount. The reversal of the accrual reduces the expense sub-account.

4. **Insurance or Warranty Claims:** If the organization files insurance claims or receives reimbursements for warranty costs, the expense sub-accounts decrease. This decrease occurs when the organization receives the insurance settlement or warranty reimbursement, reducing the previously recognized expense for the claim or warranty provision.

5. **Cost Recoveries:** If the organization is able to recover costs previously incurred, the expense sub-accounts decrease. This can happen when the organization receives reimbursements or offsets from third parties for certain expenses, reducing the net cost incurred.

6. **Cost Allocation Adjustments:** In some cases, cost allocation methods or estimates may change, resulting in adjustments to previously allocated expenses. This can happen when there are changes in

the allocation basis, cost drivers, or accounting policies. The adjustments decrease the previously allocated expenses in the respective sub-accounts.

It's important to note that the specific accounts and sub-accounts used to track expenses can vary depending on the organization's chart of accounts and accounting policies. The decrease in expense sub-accounts occurs as a result of the appropriate recording and recognition of the expense adjustments or events in accordance with generally accepted accounting principles (GAAP) or other applicable accounting standards.

Sample journal entries for the given transactions as examples:
Asset Transactions:

a. Purchase of equipment for $5,000, paid in cash. **Equipment $5,000 Cash $5,000**

b. Sale of inventory for $2,000, received in cash. **Cash $2,000 Sales Revenue $2,000 Cost of Goods Sold (To record cost of inventory sold)**

c. Acquisition of a building through a mortgage loan of $100,000. **Building $100,000 Mortgage Payable $100,000**

d. Payment of $1,200 for insurance coverage for the next 12 months. **Prepaid Insurance $1,200 Cash $1,200**

e. Purchase of $500 of office supplies on credit. **Office Supplies $500 Accounts Payable $500**

f. Collection of $10,000 accounts receivable from a customer. **Cash $10,000 Accounts Receivable $10,000**

g. Investment in stocks of another company for $3,000. **Investments $3,000 Cash $3,000**

h. Depreciation expense of $500 recorded for the month. **Depreciation Expense $500 Accumulated Depreciation $50**

Liability Transactions:

a. Payment of $2,000 accounts payable to a supplier. **Accounts Payable $2,000 Cash $2,000**

b. Borrowing $50,000 from a bank. Cash $50,000 Notes Payable $50,000

c. Payment of $1,000 interest on a loan. Interest Expense $1,000 Cash $1,000

d. Accrual of $1,500 salaries payable to employees. Salaries Expense $1,500 Salaries Payable $1,500

e. Issuance of bonds worth $1,000,000 to raise capital. Cash $1,000,000 Bonds Payable $1,000,000

f. Payment of $2,000 in taxes to the government. Taxes Payable $2,000 Cash $2,000

g. Recognition of a warranty liability of $3,500 for products sold. Warranty Expense $3,500 Warranty Liability $3,500

h. Repayment of a $10,000 loan principal. Notes Payable $10,000 Cash $10,000

Owners' Equity Transactions:

a. Initial investment of $50,000 by the owner into the business. Cash $50,000 Capital $50,000

b. Declaration of $5,000 dividends to shareholders. Dividends $5,000 Retained Earnings $5,000

c. Issuance of 1,000 additional shares to investors at $10 per share. Cash $10,000 Common Stock $10,000

d. Net income of $20,000 for the period. Retained Earnings $20,000 Income $20,000

e. Transfer of $2,500 net income to retained earnings. Retained Earnings $2,500 Income $2,500

f. Revaluation of fixed assets resulting in a $5,000 increase in owners' equity. Fixed Assets $5,000 Revaluation Surplus $5,000

g. Recognition of a $1,500 loss on the sale of an investment. Loss on Investment $1,500 Investments $1,500

h. Reinvestment of $3,000 earnings into the business.
Cash $3,000 Retained Earnings $3,000

These journal entries represent simplified examples of how various transactions could be journalized. Keep in mind that the specific accounts and amounts may vary depending on the company's accounting policies and chart of accounts. It's essential to consult accounting standards and company-specific guidelines when recording actual transactions.

Here's an extended explanation of how each transaction is posted to the general ledger:
1. Purchase of equipment for $5,000, paid in cash.
   Equipment Account:
   - Debit: $5,000
   - Credit: Not applicable
   Cash Account:
   - Debit: Not applicable
   - Credit: $5,000

   Explanation: The equipment account is debited with $5,000 to increase the equipment's value. Since cash is used for the purchase, the cash account is credited with $5,000, reflecting a decrease in cash.

2. Payment of $2,000 accounts payable to a supplier.
   Accounts Payable Account:
   - Debit: Not applicable
   - Credit: $2,000
   Cash Account:
   - Debit: $2,000
   - Credit: Not applicable

Explanation: The accounts payable account is credited with $2,000 to reduce the outstanding liability owed to the supplier. Simultaneously, the cash account is debited with $2,000 to record the cash outflow for the payment.

3. Sale of inventory for $2,000, received in cash. Cash Account:
   - Debit: $2,000
   - Credit: Not applicable

   Sales Revenue Account:
   - Debit: Not applicable
   - Credit: $2,000

   Cost of Goods Sold Account:
   - Debit: $X (cost of inventory sold)
   - Credit: Not applicable

   Explanation: The cash account is debited with $2,000 to record the cash inflow from the sale. The sales revenue account is credited with $2,000, reflecting the revenue generated from the sale. Additionally, the cost of goods sold account is debited with the cost associated with the inventory sold.

4. Initial investment of $50,000 by the owner into the business. Cash Account:
   - Debit: $50,000
   - Credit: Not applicable

   Capital Account:
   - Debit: Not applicable
   - Credit: $50,000

Explanation: The cash account is debited with $50,000 to record the increase in cash due to the owner's investment. Simultaneously, the capital account is credited with $50,000, reflecting the owner's equity in the business.

These examples demonstrate how each transaction is posted to the general ledger. Each account affected by the transaction is identified, and the corresponding debits and credits are recorded accordingly. This process ensures that the accounting equation (Assets = Liabilities + Equity) remains balanced. It's important to note that these examples provide a simplified illustration, and actual transactions may involve additional accounts and complexities based on the specific nature of the business operations.

CHAPTER FIVE
What is A General Ledger?

The general ledger is a core component of the accounting system that serves as a central repository for recording and organizing financial transactions. It is an essential tool used by businesses to maintain accurate and detailed records of their financial activities. In this book, we will examine the concept of the general ledger, its purpose, and its significance in financial accounting.

The general ledger is a comprehensive record of all the accounts used by a company. It contains individual account entries for assets, liabilities, equity, revenue, and expenses. Each account within the general ledger represents a specific aspect of the business's financial position or performance. For example, there may be separate accounts for cash, accounts payable, accounts receivable, inventory, sales revenue, salaries expense, and more.

The primary purpose of the general ledger is to provide a complete and organized view of a company's financial transactions. It serves as a central hub where all financial information is recorded, making it easier for accountants and auditors to analyze and interpret the data. By keeping track of all transactions, the general ledger enables businesses to generate accurate financial statements, such as the balance sheet, income statement, and cash flow statement.

Recording transactions in the general ledger involves a process known as posting. When a transaction occurs, it is initially recorded in the appropriate subsidiary journal, such as the sales journal, cash receipts journal, or purchases journal. The information from these subsidiary journals is then transferred or posted to the corresponding accounts in the general ledger. This ensures that each transaction is properly classified and reflected in the appropriate accounts.

The general ledger provides several benefits to businesses:

1. **Accuracy and Reliability:** By maintaining a detailed record of financial transactions, the general ledger ensures accuracy and reliability in the financial information. It serves as a source of truth for the company's financial position, enabling management and stakeholders to make informed decisions based on reliable data.

2. **Financial Reporting:** The general ledger serves as the foundation for generating financial statements. It provides the necessary information to prepare balance sheets, income statements, and cash flow statements, which are crucial for assessing a company's financial performance and meeting reporting requirements.

3. **Analysis and Decision-Making:** The general ledger allows accountants, financial analysts, and management to analyze financial data and identify trends, patterns, and insights. It provides a comprehensive view of the company's financial health, allowing for informed decision-making and strategic planning.

4. **Compliance and Auditing:** The general ledger plays a critical role in regulatory compliance and auditing. It provides a detailed trail of financial transactions, making it easier to demonstrate compliance with accounting standards and regulations. Additionally, auditors rely on the general ledger to examine and verify the accuracy of financial records during the auditing process.

5. **Historical Record:** The general ledger serves as a historical record of a company's financial transactions. It enables businesses to track and reference past transactions, facilitating historical analysis, performance comparisons, and future forecasting.

The general ledger is a fundamental component of the accounting system. It serves as a centralized repository for recording and organizing financial transactions, ensuring accuracy, reliability, and compliance. By maintaining a detailed and up-to-date general ledger, businesses can generate accurate financial statements, analyze financial data, make informed decisions, and meet reporting requirements. It is an indispensable tool in financial accounting that contributes to the overall success and transparency of a business.

The general ledger is a cornerstone of the accounting process, serving as the central repository for all financial transactions within an organization. It is a comprehensive record that contains individual accounts, each representing a specific aspect of the company's financial activity. In this article, we will explore the general ledger in detail, its purpose, structure, and significance in maintaining accurate financial records.

The structure of the general ledger is based on the chart of accounts, which is a systematic listing of all the accounts used by an organization. The chart of accounts is typically organized in a hierarchical manner, with major categories such as assets, liabilities, equity, revenue, and expenses. Each category is further broken down into sub-accounts, creating a detailed framework to record and classify transactions accurately.

Each account in the general ledger has a unique identifier, often referred to as an account number or code. This identifier helps in identifying and locating specific accounts within the ledger. Additionally, each account has two sides: the debit side and the credit side. Debits and credits are used to record increases and decreases in account balances, respectively.

Recording Transactions in the General Ledger: Every financial transaction that occurs within an organization is recorded in the general ledger using a process called journal entry. A journal entry includes the date of the transaction, the accounts affected, and the corresponding debits and credits. The entry is then posted to the appropriate accounts in the general ledger, updating the account balances accordingly.

For example, when a company makes a sale, a journal entry is recorded to recognize the revenue and accounts receivable. The revenue account is credited to increase the revenue balance, while the accounts receivable account is debited to increase the asset balance. These entries are posted to their respective accounts in the general ledger, reflecting the impact of the transaction.

Maintaining Accuracy and Integrity: The accuracy and integrity of the general ledger are of paramount importance to ensure reliable financial reporting. Several control mechanisms and best practices are employed to maintain the accuracy of the ledger. These include:

1. **Segregation of Duties:** The responsibility for recording transactions, authorizing entries, and reviewing the general ledger should be divided among different individuals. This segregation of duties helps prevent errors and fraud by ensuring that no single person has complete control over the accounting process.

2. **Reconciliation:** Regular reconciliation of the general ledger accounts with external sources, such as bank statements and supplier statements, is essential. Reconciliation helps identify any discrepancies or errors, ensuring that the ledger balances accurately reflect the actual financial position of the organization.

3. **Documentation:** Proper documentation of transactions is critical for maintaining the integrity of the general ledger. Supporting documents, such as invoices, receipts, and contracts, should be filed and referenced appropriately. This documentation provides evidence of the validity and authenticity of the recorded transactions.

4. **Review and Audit:** Periodic reviews of the general ledger by management or internal auditors are essential to identify and rectify errors or inconsistencies promptly. External audits by independent auditors also play a vital role in ensuring the accuracy and compliance of the financial records.

Reporting and Financial Analysis: The general ledger is a valuable source of information for financial reporting and analysis. It provides the necessary data to prepare financial statements, including the balance sheet, income statement, and statement of cash flows. These statements provide a comprehensive view of an organization's financial performance, position, and liquidity.

Financial analysis involves examining the data in the general ledger to gain insights into various aspects of the organization's financial health. Ratios, trends, and comparisons are used to assess profitability, efficiency, liquidity, and solvency. By analyzing the general ledger data, stakeholders can make informed decisions, evaluate performance, and identify areas for improvement.

The general ledger is a crucial component of the accounting process, serving as a comprehensive record of financial transactions. It plays a vital role in financial reporting, analysis, and decision-making. By maintaining accurate and reliable general ledger records, organizations can ensure transparency, compliance, and effective management of their financial resources.

CHAPTER SIX
Accountants Worksheets

Accountants and auditors often use worksheets as a valuable tool to facilitate the preparation and analysis of financial information. Worksheets provide a structured framework for organizing data, performing calculations, and documenting supporting details. They offer several benefits that contribute to accurate financial reporting, efficient analysis, and effective audit procedures. Here are eight examples of how accountants and auditors use worksheets:

1. **Trial Balance Preparation:** Accountants use worksheets to prepare trial balances, which summarize the balances of all accounts in the general ledger. A worksheet allows for the systematic listing of account names, debits, credits, and balances, making it easier to identify any discrepancies or errors.

2. **Adjusting Entries:** Worksheets are essential for making adjusting entries at the end of an accounting period. They provide a clear format for recording and documenting adjustments related to accruals, deferrals, estimates, and corrections. Accountants can input the original account balances, make necessary adjustments, and calculate the adjusted balances.

3. **Financial Statement Preparation:** Accountants utilize worksheets to prepare financial statements, such as the income statement, balance sheet, and cash

flow statement. Worksheets help organize the financial data required for each statement, including revenues, expenses, assets, liabilities, and equity. They enable the calculation of key financial ratios and the consolidation of multiple worksheets for consolidated financial statements.

4. **Budgeting and Forecasting:** Worksheets are commonly used for budgeting and forecasting purposes. Accountants can create separate worksheets to input projected revenues, expenses, and other financial variables. These worksheets allow for easy comparison of actual results with the budgeted amounts, facilitating variance analysis and performance evaluation.

5. **Ratio Analysis:** Accountants and financial analysts use worksheets to perform ratio analysis, which involves calculating and interpreting various financial ratios to assess a company's financial health and performance. Worksheets provide a structured format to input the relevant financial data and compute ratios, such as liquidity ratios, profitability ratios, and efficiency ratios.

6. **Audit Documentation:** Auditors use worksheets as part of their audit documentation. They document their audit procedures, findings, and conclusions in worksheets, providing a clear and organized record of their work. Worksheets serve as a reference for future audits and help maintain a proper audit trail.

7. **Internal Controls Evaluation:** Worksheets are useful for evaluating internal controls within an organization. Accountants and auditors can create worksheets to document control activities, identify control weaknesses or deficiencies, and propose remedial actions. This systematic approach helps strengthen internal controls and mitigate risks.

8. **Data Analysis and Reconciliation:** Worksheets facilitate data analysis and reconciliation processes. Accountants and auditors can use worksheets to compare financial data from different sources, identify discrepancies, and investigate the underlying causes. Worksheets also help in reconciling accounts, such as bank reconciliations or intercompany reconciliations, by systematically listing the items to be reconciled and providing space for explanations.

Accountants and auditors use worksheets for a variety of purposes, including trial balance preparation, adjusting entries, financial statement preparation, budgeting and forecasting, ratio analysis, audit documentation, internal controls evaluation, and data analysis and reconciliation. Worksheets provide a structured format for organizing financial data, performing calculations, documenting supporting details, and facilitating analysis and review. They contribute to accurate financial reporting, efficient analysis, effective audit procedures, and informed decision-making. The use of worksheets enhances the overall efficiency and effectiveness of accounting and auditing processes.

Accountants' worksheets are valuable tools used in the accounting profession to organize, analyze, and adjust financial data before preparing formal financial statements. These worksheets provide a structured framework for accountants to make adjustments, perform calculations, and ensure accuracy in the final financial reporting. In this article, we will delve into the purpose, components, and benefits of accountant's worksheets in streamlining the accounting process.

The primary purpose of accountants' worksheets is to facilitate the preparation and adjustment of financial statements. They serve as an intermediary step between the general ledger and the formal financial statements. Accountants use worksheets to gather data, make adjusting entries, analyze accounts, and compute financial ratios, ensuring the accuracy and completeness of the financial information.

Components of Accountants Worksheets:

1. **Trial Balance:** The trial balance is often the starting point of an accountant's worksheet. It is a listing of all the accounts and their respective balances from the general ledger. The trial balance serves as a basis for verifying the equality of total debits and credits and acts as a reference for subsequent adjustments.

2. **Adjusting Entries**: Accountants use worksheets to record and calculate adjusting entries. Adjusting entries are necessary to recognize accrued revenues or expenses, prepaid expenses, unearned revenues, depreciation, and other items that need to be properly

allocated to the appropriate accounting period. The worksheets provide a space for accountants to document these adjustments and ensure that they are accurately reflected in the financial statements.

3. **Supporting Calculations:** Accountants worksheets include sections for performing various calculations and analyses. These calculations may involve computing depreciation expense, interest expense, inventory valuation, and other financial metrics. Worksheets allow accountants to organize and present these calculations clearly, making it easier to review and verify the accuracy of the results.

4. **Financial Ratios:** Accountants often use worksheets to compute financial ratios. These ratios provide insights into the financial health and performance of a company. By comparing current ratios, debt-to-equity ratios, profitability ratios, and other key metrics, accountants can assess the company's liquidity, solvency, profitability, and efficiency. Worksheets provide a structured format for performing these calculations and analyzing the results.

Benefits of Accountants Worksheets:

1. **Organization and Efficiency:** Accountants worksheets provide a structured framework for organizing financial data. They streamline the accounting process by providing a clear format for recording and analyzing information. By having designated sections for different tasks, worksheets

help accountants work more efficiently and reduce the chances of errors or omissions.

2. **Accuracy and Integrity:** Accountants worksheets play a crucial role in ensuring the accuracy and integrity of financial reporting. They provide a platform for making necessary adjustments and reconciling accounts. By carefully analyzing and reviewing the data in the worksheets, accountants can identify discrepancies, resolve errors, and reconcile account balances, leading to more accurate financial statements.

3. **Documentation and Audit Trail:** Accountants worksheets serve as a documentation tool, capturing the adjustments and calculations made during the accounting process. They provide a comprehensive record of the steps taken to prepare the financial statements, including supporting calculations and explanations. These worksheets serve as an audit trail, allowing auditors to review and verify the accuracy of the financial statements.

4. **Analysis and Decision-Making:** Accountants worksheets facilitate financial analysis and decision-making. By performing calculations and computing ratios within the worksheets, accountants can gain insights into the company's financial performance and identify areas of concern or improvement. The organized format of the worksheets helps present the data in a digestible manner, supporting effective decision-making by management and other stakeholders.

5. **Collaboration and Communication:** Accountants worksheets can serve as a communication tool between different departments within an organization. They allow accountants to share information and collaborate with colleagues, auditors, and financial analysts. Worksheets provide a structured format for presenting financial data and explanations, enhancing communication and understanding among team members.

Accountants' worksheets are vital tools in the accounting process, providing a structured framework for organizing, analyzing, and adjusting financial data. They streamline the preparation of financial statements, ensure accuracy and integrity, support financial analysis, and facilitate effective decision-making. Accountants rely on worksheets to document adjustments, perform calculations, and provide a clear audit trail for the accounting process. By leveraging the benefits of accountants' worksheets, accountants can streamline their work and produce accurate and reliable financial statements.

CPA (Certified Public Accountant) firms play a crucial role in providing professional accounting services, including auditing, tax preparation, and financial advisory. To ensure efficiency and accuracy in their work, CPA firms often utilize accountant's worksheets as valuable tools in their accounting processes. These worksheets help streamline data organization, analysis, and adjustment, ultimately leading to more reliable and comprehensive financial reporting. In this article, we will explore the relationship between CPA firms and accountant's worksheets, highlighting their benefits and importance in the accounting profession.

Streamlining Data Organization:

One of the primary functions of accountants' worksheets is to streamline the organization of financial data. For CPA firms dealing with numerous clients and complex financial information, worksheets provide a structured format for gathering, categorizing, and storing data. These worksheets typically include sections for trial balances, adjusting entries, supporting calculations, and financial ratios, allowing accountants to organize and track financial data efficiently. By implementing standardized worksheets, CPA firms can ensure consistency across different clients and engagements, promoting efficiency and reducing the risk of errors or omissions.

Facilitating Data Analysis and Adjustment:

Accountant's worksheets enable CPA firms to perform critical data analysis and adjustment tasks. These worksheets provide designated sections for making adjusting entries, which are necessary to account for accruals, deferrals, depreciation, and other adjustments that ensure accurate financial reporting. By utilizing worksheets, accountants can record and document these adjustments systematically, making it easier to review, analyze, and ensure compliance with accounting standards.

Furthermore, accountants' worksheets offer a platform for performing various calculations and financial analysis. CPA firms can use these worksheets to compute financial ratios, analyze trends, and conduct ratio analysis, which provides valuable insights into the financial health and performance of their clients. The structured format of the worksheets enhances the accuracy and reliability of these calculations, supporting more informed decision-making for both the CPA firm and their clients.

Supporting Audit and Assurance:

CPA firms are often engaged in auditing and assurance services, where they independently examine and verify the financial statements of their clients. Accountants' worksheets play a critical role in supporting these activities. During an audit engagement, accountants use worksheets to document and track their audit procedures, including reconciliations, account analysis, and substantive testing. The worksheets serve as an audit trail, providing evidence of the work performed and supporting the findings and conclusions of the audit.

Moreover, accountant's worksheets facilitate the communication and collaboration between the audit team members. These worksheets can be shared and updated by different team members, allowing for a more efficient and coordinated audit process. The structured format of the worksheets ensures that the information is organized and easily accessible, promoting effective communication and knowledge sharing within the CPA firm.

Enhancing Accuracy and Quality Control:

Accountant's worksheets are instrumental in enhancing the accuracy and quality control processes within CPA firms.

These worksheets provide a standardized format for recording and documenting adjustments, calculations, and analysis. They also serve as a reference point for reviewing the work performed, allowing for effective quality control checks. The structured nature of the worksheets ensures that all necessary steps and procedures are followed, reducing the risk of errors or oversights.

Furthermore, accountants' worksheets support the implementation of internal control procedures within CPA firms. By using standardized worksheets, firms can enforce segregation of duties, where different team members are responsible for different aspects of the worksheet preparation and review process. This segregation helps maintain the integrity and reliability of the financial information, providing assurance to clients and stakeholders.

CPA firms heavily rely on accountants' worksheets to streamline their accounting processes, enhance efficiency, and ensure accuracy in financial reporting. These worksheets facilitate data organization, analysis, and adjustment, providing a structured format for recording, calculating, and documenting financial information. By utilizing accountants' worksheets, CPA firms can enhance their ability to deliver reliable and comprehensive financial services, including auditing, tax preparation, and financial advisory. Ultimately, the integration of accountant's worksheets in the accounting processes of CPA firms contributes to the provision of high-quality services and the maintenance of professional standards in the accounting profession.

CHAPTER SEVEN
Charts of Accounts

A chart of accounts is a structured list of all the individual accounts used by a business to record its financial transactions. It provides a systematic and organized framework for categorizing and classifying financial activities, making it easier to track, analyze, and report on the company's financial information.

The chart of accounts typically consists of a numerical or alphanumeric coding system that assigns a unique identifier to each account. This coding system helps in categorizing the accounts based on their nature, such as assets, liabilities, equity, revenue, and expenses. By using a standardized chart of accounts, businesses can ensure consistency in financial reporting and facilitate easier data analysis across different departments and entities.

Preparing a chart of accounts involves careful consideration of the specific needs and structure of the business. While the exact accounts and their numbering may vary depending on the industry and company, there are some common accounts found in most charts of accounts.

Here are a few examples:

1. **Assets:**
   - Cash: Represents the amount of money available in the company's bank accounts.
   - Accounts Receivable: Tracks the amounts owed to the company by its customers.

174

- Inventory: Records the value of goods held by the company for sale.
- Property, Plant, and Equipment: Captures the value of tangible assets such as buildings, machinery, and vehicles.

2. **Liabilities:**
   - Accounts Payable: Tracks the amounts owed by the company to its suppliers and vendors.
   - Loans Payable: Records any outstanding loans or borrowings.
   - Accrued Expenses: Represents expenses that have been incurred but not yet paid.

3. **Equity:**
   - Share Capital: Represents the value of the company's shares issued to shareholders.
   - Retained Earnings: Tracks the accumulated profits or losses of the company over time.

4. **Revenue:**
   - Sales: Records the revenue generated from the sale of goods or services.
   - Interest Income: Captures any interest earned on investments or loans.

5. **Expenses:**
   - Salaries and Wages: Represents the cost of employee compensation.
   - Rent Expense: Records the rent paid for office or business premises.
   - Utilities Expense: Tracks the cost of utilities such as electricity and water.

When preparing a chart of accounts, it is important to consider the specific needs of the business. The chart of accounts should be tailored to reflect the company's unique operations, industry-specific requirements, and reporting needs. It should also allow for scalability and flexibility to accommodate future growth or changes in the business.

Here is an example of a simplified chart of accounts for a retail business:

- Assets: 1000 Cash 1100 Accounts Receivable 1200 Inventory 1300 Furniture and Fixtures
- Liabilities: 2000 Accounts Payable 2100 Loans Payable
- Equity: 3000 Share Capital 3100 Retained Earnings
- Revenue: 4000 Sales 4100 Interest Income
- Expenses: 5000 Salaries and Wages 5100 Rent Expense 5200 Utilities Expense

This is just a basic example, and in practice, the chart of accounts may include many more accounts based on the specific needs of the business. The numbering system allows for easy identification and classification of accounts, making it simpler to track and analyze financial transactions.

A chart of accounts is a vital tool in financial accounting that helps organize and classify a company's financial transactions. It provides a structured framework for recording, tracking, and reporting financial information, allowing businesses to effectively manage their finances and make informed decisions. By customizing the chart of accounts to suit the specific needs of the business, companies can enhance financial reporting, streamline data analysis, and ensure consistency in financial operations.

Importance and Benefits of Charts of Accounts

The chart of accounts is a fundamental component of the accounting system used by organizations to categorize, record, and report financial transactions. It serves as a standardized framework that organizes and classifies various accounts, providing a systematic structure for tracking financial information. In this article, we will explore the importance, structure, and benefits of charts of accounts in building the foundation for accurate financial reporting.

Importance of Charts of Accounts:

1. **Consistency and Standardization:** The chart of accounts ensures consistency and standardization in financial reporting across an organization. By providing a uniform structure for organizing accounts, it enables consistent recording and classification of financial transactions. This uniformity is crucial for accurate and reliable financial reporting, both within the organization and for external stakeholders.

2. **Financial Analysis and Decision-Making:** A well-structured chart of accounts enables effective financial analysis and decision-making. By categorizing accounts into different groups, such as assets, liabilities, equity, revenue, and expenses, it allows for easy identification and examination of specific financial components. This categorization facilitates the calculation of financial ratios, trend analysis, and comparison of financial performance, enabling stakeholders to make informed decisions.

3. **Regulatory Compliance:** Charts of accounts help organizations comply with accounting and reporting standards. By following a standardized chart of accounts, organizations ensure that their financial statements are prepared in accordance with the applicable regulatory requirements. This compliance promotes transparency and accountability, enhancing trust and confidence among stakeholders.

Structure of Charts of Accounts:

A chart of accounts typically consists of a hierarchical structure that organizes accounts into different levels. The structure may vary depending on the organization's size, complexity, and industry. The general structure includes:

1. **Account Categories:** The highest level of the chart of accounts typically includes broad account categories, such as assets, liabilities, equity, revenue, and expenses. These categories represent the major financial components of an organization.

2. **Account Groups:** Within each category, further classification is done into account groups. For example, under the asset category, there may be account groups such as current assets, fixed assets, and intangible assets. These groups help in organizing accounts based on their nature and characteristics.

3. **Accounts:** Accounts represent the specific items or elements within each account group. Examples of

accounts include cash, accounts receivable, accounts payable, salaries expense, sales revenue, and inventory. Each account is assigned a unique account number or code for identification and reference purposes.

Benefits of Charts of Accounts:

1. **Accurate Financial Reporting:** A well-designed chart of accounts ensures accurate and consistent financial reporting. By providing a standardized structure, it facilitates the recording, classification, and presentation of financial transactions. This consistency enhances the accuracy and reliability of financial statements, enabling organizations to meet their reporting obligations.

2. **Efficient Data Analysis:** The chart of accounts supports efficient data analysis by providing a logical framework for organizing financial information. It allows for quick identification and retrieval of specific accounts, enabling stakeholders to analyze and interpret financial data effectively. This efficiency in data analysis helps in decision-making, financial planning, and performance evaluation.

3. **Scalability and Flexibility:** A well-structured chart of accounts accommodates the changing needs and growth of an organization. It allows for the addition or modification of accounts as the organization expands or adapts to new business requirements. This scalability and flexibility ensure that the chart

of accounts remains relevant and applicable over time.

4. **Integration with Accounting Systems:** The chart of accounts serves as the foundation for integrating accounting systems and software. It provides a framework for mapping and aligning financial transactions within the system, ensuring the accuracy and integrity of data across different modules. This integration streamlines the accounting process and enhances efficiency in data processing and reporting.

Charts of accounts are essential tools for organizing, categorizing, and reporting financial transactions. They provide a standardized framework that ensures consistency, accuracy, and compliance in financial reporting. A well-structured chart of accounts enables efficient data analysis, supports decision-making, and facilitates regulatory compliance. By building a strong foundation through a comprehensive chart of accounts, organizations can enhance their financial reporting capabilities and provide reliable and meaningful information to stakeholders.

Structured Framework – Charts of Accounts

In addition to providing a structured framework for organizing financial transactions, charts of accounts offer further benefits in terms of financial analysis, reporting, and customization. In this article, we will delve deeper into these aspects, highlighting how charts of accounts can be tailored to meet specific organizational needs and improve financial management.

Financial Analysis and Performance Evaluation:

A well-designed chart of accounts enables organizations to perform detailed financial analysis and evaluate their performance. By categorizing accounts into specific groups and subgroups, the chart of accounts allows for granular analysis of different financial components. For example, within the revenue category, accounts may be classified by product lines, geographical regions, or customer segments, providing insights into profitability by these specific factors.

The chart of accounts also supports the calculation of financial ratios and key performance indicators (KPIs). With a properly structured chart of accounts, it becomes easier to calculate ratios such as current ratio, debt-to-equity ratio, return on investment (ROI), and gross profit margin. These ratios provide valuable insights into liquidity, solvency, efficiency, and profitability, helping stakeholders assess the financial health and performance of the organization.

Customization and Scalability:

Charts of accounts can be customized to meet the specific needs of an organization. This customization involves tailoring the structure and accounts to reflect the unique characteristics and operations of the business. For example, an organization in the retail industry may have specific accounts for inventory, cost of goods sold (COGS), and sales by product category or department.

Customization also allows for scalability as the organization grows or evolves. Additional accounts and categories can be added to accommodate new business lines, subsidiaries, or revenue streams. This flexibility ensures that the chart of accounts remains relevant and adaptable to changing circumstances, providing a robust foundation for financial reporting and analysis.

Reporting and Decision-Making:

The chart of accounts plays a crucial role in financial reporting. It provides a systematic structure for recording financial transactions, making it easier to prepare accurate and comprehensive financial statements. With a well-organized chart of accounts, organizations can generate reports that summarize financial data by category, group, or specific accounts. These reports help stakeholders understand the financial position, performance, and cash flow of the organization.

The chart of accounts also facilitates effective decision-making. By providing a clear categorization of accounts, it enables managers and executives to analyze financial information and make informed decisions. For example, by reviewing expense accounts, management can identify cost-saving opportunities or areas where resources can be allocated more effectively.

Compliance and Audit:

A well-maintained chart of accounts helps ensure compliance with accounting standards and facilitates audits. By following a standardized chart of accounts, organizations can ensure that their financial statements adhere to the required reporting guidelines. This compliance promotes transparency, comparability, and accountability.

During audits, the chart of accounts serves as a key reference point for auditors. It provides the necessary structure and organization for auditors to review and assess the accuracy and reliability of financial transactions. The chart of accounts, along with supporting documentation, serves as an audit trail, facilitating the audit process and ensuring transparency.

Charts of accounts serve as the foundation for accurate financial analysis, reporting, and decision-making. They enable organizations to analyze financial data, evaluate performance, and customize the structure to meet specific needs. By utilizing a well-structured chart of accounts, organizations can enhance their financial management processes, comply with accounting standards, and provide meaningful insights to stakeholders.

CHAPTER EIGHT
Financial Accounting Equation - ALORE

ALORE is an acronym that stands for Assets, Liabilities, Owner's Equity, Revenues, and Expenses. It is a framework used in financial accounting to categorize and classify the various elements that are reported in a company's financial statements.

1. **Assets:** Assets are economic resources owned or controlled by a business that have the potential to generate future economic benefits. They represent the value that a company possesses. Examples of assets include cash, accounts receivable, inventory, property, plant, and equipment, and investments. Assets are classified into current assets and non-current (or long-term) assets based on their expected conversion to cash within a year.

2. **Liabilities:** Liabilities are obligations or debts that a company owes to external parties. They represent the company's financial obligations or responsibilities. Examples of liabilities include accounts payable, loans payable, accrued expenses, and deferred revenue. Liabilities are categorized into current liabilities and non-current (or long-term) liabilities based on their maturity date.

3. **Owner's Equity:** Owner's Equity represents the residual interest in the assets of a company after deducting liabilities. It represents the ownership interest of the company's shareholders or owners.

Owner's Equity includes the initial capital contributed by the owners plus retained earnings, which are the accumulated profits or losses of the company over time.

4. **Revenues:** Revenues are the inflows of assets or settlements of liabilities that result from the ordinary activities of a company. They represent the company's earnings or income generated from selling goods, providing services, or other operating activities. Revenues increase the owner's equity and are typically recognized when they are earned, regardless of when the cash is received.

5. **Expenses:** Expenses are the outflows of assets or incurrence of liabilities that arise from the company's efforts to generate revenues. They represent the costs or expenses incurred in running the business. Examples of expenses include salaries and wages, rent, utilities, raw materials, marketing expenses, and depreciation. Expenses decrease the owner's equity and are recognized when the related revenue is earned or when the expenses are incurred.

The **ALORE** framework serves as a foundation for financial accounting. It provides a systematic way to organize and classify the financial transactions and events of a company, ensuring that all relevant information is captured and reported accurately in the financial statements. By categorizing elements into these five categories, it allows for consistency and comparability in financial reporting, enabling stakeholders to analyze and assess the financial position and performance of a company.

The basic accounting equation, also known as the balance sheet equation, is a fundamental concept in accounting that represents the relationship between a company's assets, liabilities, and owner's equity. The equation is as follows:

Assets = Liabilities + Owner's Equity

This equation expresses the principle that a company's total assets are financed by either debt (liabilities) or the owner's investment (owner's equity). Here is an explanation of each component of the equation:

1. **Assets:** Assets represent the economic resources owned or controlled by a company that have future economic value. They can include cash, accounts receivable, inventory, property, plant, equipment, investments, and other tangible or intangible assets. Assets are recorded on the balance sheet and provide the basis for generating revenues.

2. **Liabilities:** Liabilities are the company's obligations or debts to external parties. They represent amounts owed to creditors, suppliers, lenders, or other stakeholders. Liabilities can include accounts payable, loans payable, accrued expenses, and deferred revenue. Liabilities reflect the company's financial obligations and are also recorded on the balance sheet.

3. **Owner's Equity:** Owner's Equity represents the residual interest in the assets of a company after deducting liabilities. It represents the ownership claim of the company's shareholders or owners.

Owner's Equity includes the initial capital contributed by the owners and any additional investments made, as well as retained earnings, which are the accumulated profits or losses over time. Owner's Equity is also reported on the balance sheet.

The basic accounting equation ensures that the financial records of a company are in balance. It implies that the total value of a company's assets is equal to the total of its liabilities and owner's equity. In other words, a company's assets are funded by either borrowing (liabilities) or the owner's investment (owner's equity). This equation serves as the foundation for the double-entry bookkeeping system, where every transaction is recorded with at least two entries to maintain the balance of the accounting equation.

Extended Accounting Equation

The extended version of the basic accounting equation takes into account additional elements that impact a company's financial position. It expands the equation to incorporate revenue, expenses, gains, and losses. The extended accounting equation is as follows:

Assets = Liabilities + Owner's Equity + Revenues - Expenses + Gains - Losses

Let's explain each component of the extended accounting equation:

1. **Assets:** Assets represent the economic resources owned or controlled by a company that have future

economic value. They include cash, accounts receivable, inventory, property, plant, equipment, and other tangible or intangible assets.

2. **Liabilities:** Liabilities are the company's obligations or debts to external parties. They include accounts payable, loans payable, accrued expenses, and other amounts owed to creditors, suppliers, or lenders.

3. **Owner's Equity:** Owner's Equity represents the residual interest in the assets of a company after deducting liabilities. It includes the initial capital contributed by the owners and any additional investments made, as well as retained earnings.

4. **Revenues:** Revenues are the inflows of assets or settlements of liabilities that result from the ordinary activities of a company. They represent the company's earnings or income generated from selling goods, providing services, or other operating activities.

5. **Expenses:** Expenses are the outflows of assets or incurrence of liabilities that arise from the company's efforts to generate revenues. They represent the costs or expenses incurred in running the business.

6. **Gains:** Gains are the positive financial outcomes from non-operating activities, such as the sale of assets, investments, or other transactions that are not part of the company's core operations.

7. **Losses:** Losses are the negative financial outcomes from non-operating activities, such as write-offs, impairments, or losses incurred from the disposal of assets or investments.

By including revenues, expenses, gains, and losses in the equation, the extended version provides a more comprehensive view of a company's financial position. It reflects the impact of the company's operating and non-operating activities on its assets, liabilities, and owner's equity. This expanded equation helps to assess the company's overall performance and the effect of different transactions on its financial statements. The sub-accounts of assets can vary depending on the specific chart of accounts used by a business. However, here are some common sub-accounts of assets that you may encounter:

1. Current Assets:
   - Cash and Cash Equivalents
   - Accounts Receivable
   - Inventory
   - Prepaid Expenses
   - Short-term Investments
   - Marketable Securities
2. Fixed Assets:
   - Land
   - Buildings
   - Machinery and Equipment
   - Vehicles
   - Furniture and Fixtures
   - Accumulated Depreciation
3. Intangible Assets:

- Goodwill
- Patents
- Trademarks
- Copyrights
- Brand Value
- Software
4. Investments:
    - Long-term Investments
    - Equity Investments
    - Bonds and Notes Receivable
    - Mutual Funds
    - Stocks and Securities
    - Investment Property
5. Other Assets:
    - Deferred Tax Assets
    - Prepaid Expenses
    - Deposits
    - Advances to Suppliers or Employees
    - Restricted Cash
    - Non-current Portion of Prepaid Expenses

It's important to note that these sub-accounts are just examples, and businesses can have different account classifications and sub-categories based on their specific needs and industry requirements. The chart of accounts can be customized to suit the particular nature of the organization's assets and to provide detailed information for financial reporting and analysis.

Integration of ALORE with Financial Elements:

The ALORE framework complements and intersects with the financial elements of a business. Accounting practices, encompassed within ALORE, are crucial for accurately recording and managing assets, liabilities, owners' equity, revenue, and expenses. Proper legal guidance, a part of ALORE, ensures compliance with regulations and safeguards the financial interests of the business. Effective operations, risk management, and employment practices, also integral to ALORE, contribute to the financial stability, efficiency, and growth of the business.

By integrating ALORE with the financial elements of a business, entrepreneurs can establish a solid foundation for financial management, reporting, and decision-making. This integration enables entrepreneurs to effectively track and manage assets and liabilities, understand the value and financial position of the business through owners' equity, optimize revenue generation, and control expenses. Ultimately, the successful integration of ALORE with financial elements ensures the overall financial health, sustainability, and success of a business.

CHAPTER NINE
Adjusting Entries

Adjusting entries are accounting entries made at the end of an accounting period to ensure that the financial statements accurately reflect the financial position and operating results of a business. These entries are necessary because some transactions or events may not have been captured in the regular journal entries. Adjusting entries are typically made for the following reasons:

1. **Accruals:** Adjusting entries are made to record revenues or expenses that have been earned or incurred but not yet recorded. For example, if a company has provided services to a customer in one accounting period but has not yet billed the customer, an adjusting entry is made to recognize the revenue earned.

2. **Deferrals:** Adjusting entries are also made to account for cash received or paid in advance for future goods or services. For example, if a company receives cash from a customer for services that will be provided in the future, an adjusting entry is made to recognize the liability for the unearned revenue.

3. **Depreciation:** Adjusting entries are made to allocate the cost of long-term assets over their useful lives. Depreciation is a systematic allocation of the asset's cost as an expense over time. Adjusting entries for depreciation ensure that the correct portion of the

asset's cost is recognized as an expense in each accounting period.

4. **Accrued Expenses:** Adjusting entries are made to recognize expenses that have been incurred but not yet paid or recorded. For example, if a company has received services from a supplier but has not yet received the invoice, an adjusting entry is made to recognize the expense.

5. **Accrued Revenues:** Adjusting entries are also made to recognize revenues that have been earned but not yet received or recorded. For example, if a company has provided services to a customer but has not yet billed the customer, an adjusting entry is made to recognize the revenue.

Adjusting entries are necessary to ensure that the financial statements accurately reflect the financial position, results of operations, and cash flows of a business. They help to match revenues and expenses to the period in which they were earned or incurred, adhere to the accrual basis of accounting, and provide a more accurate representation of the financial performance.

Closing Entries

Closing entries are made at the end of an accounting period to transfer the balances of temporary accounts to the retained earnings or owner's equity account. Temporary accounts include revenue, expense, and dividend accounts. The purpose of closing entries is to reset the temporary accounts to zero and prepare them for the next accounting period.

Closing entries are an essential part of the accounting cycle that occurs at the end of an accounting period. They serve the purpose of resetting temporary accounts and preparing them for the next period. In this process, the temporary accounts, such as revenue, expense, and dividend accounts, are closed or zeroed out, while the balances are transferred to the retained earnings account or the appropriate equity account.

The process of closing entries involves the following steps:

1. **Close Revenue Accounts:** The balances of revenue accounts, such as sales revenue and service revenue, are transferred to the income summary account. This is done by debiting the revenue accounts and crediting the income summary account. The goal is to summarize the revenues earned during the period.

2. **Close Expense Accounts:** The balances of expense accounts, such as salaries expense and rent expense, are transferred to the income summary account. This is done by debiting the income summary account and crediting the expense accounts. The purpose is to summarize the expenses incurred during the period.

3. **Close Income Summary Account:** The balance of the income summary account, which represents the net income or net loss for the period, is transferred to the retained earnings or owner's equity account. If the income summary account has a credit balance, it is transferred by debiting the retained earnings or owner's equity account. If it has a debit balance, it is

transferred by crediting the retained earnings or owner's equity account.

4. **Close Dividend Accounts:** If the company distributes dividends to its shareholders, the balance of the dividend account is transferred to the retained earnings or owner's equity account. This is done by debiting the retained earnings or owner's equity account and crediting the dividend account.

The Main Objectives of Closing Entries:

1. **Update Retained Earnings:** Closing entries ensure that the net income or net loss for the period is properly reflected in the retained earnings account. By closing revenue and expense accounts, the net income or net loss is transferred to the retained earnings account, which helps in tracking the cumulative profits or losses of the company.

2. **Reset Temporary Accounts:** Temporary accounts, including revenue, expense, and dividend accounts, accumulate transactions for a specific accounting period. By closing these accounts, their balances are reset to zero, ready to accumulate new transactions in the next accounting period. This process ensures that each accounting period starts with a clean slate.

3. **Provide Accurate Financial Statements:** Closing entries ensure that the income statement reflects only the revenues and expenses for the current period. By transferring these balances to the retained earnings account, the income statement accurately represents

the financial performance of the company for the period.

By performing these closing entries, the temporary accounts are closed, and the financial statements are prepared with accurate balances. The next accounting period can then begin with a fresh set of temporary accounts. It's important to note that closing entries are typically recorded in the general journal and then posted to the general ledger accounts. Additionally, companies may have specific procedures and guidelines for closing entries based on their accounting policies and reporting requirements. Closing entries play a crucial role in the accounting cycle by resetting temporary accounts and updating the retained earnings account. They ensure accurate financial reporting and provide a clean start for the next accounting period. Properly executed closing entries contribute to reliable financial statements and help stakeholders assess the financial performance and position of the company.

Examples of ADJUSTING Entries in a Worksheet:

1. **Accrued Revenue:** A company has provided services to a client in December, but the payment will be received in January. To recognize the revenue in the correct period, an adjusting entry is made by debiting Accounts Receivable and crediting Service Revenue.

2. **Prepaid Expenses:** A company has paid the annual insurance premium of $12,000 in advance on January 1st. To allocate the expense over the year, an adjusting entry is made at the end of each month by

debiting Insurance Expense and crediting Prepaid Insurance ($12,000/12 months = $1,000 per month).

3. **Accrued Expenses:** A company has received utility services in December, but the bill will be received in January. To recognize the expense in the correct period, an adjusting entry is made by debiting Utility Expense and crediting Accounts Payable.

4. **Depreciation:** A company owns equipment with a useful life of five years. To allocate the cost of the equipment over its useful life, an adjusting entry is made by debiting Depreciation Expense and crediting Accumulated Depreciation. The amount is calculated based on the equipment's cost and the depreciation method used (e.g., straight-line, declining balance).

5. **Unearned Revenue:** A company receives payment in advance for a service that will be provided over the next six months. To recognize the revenue as it is earned, an adjusting entry is made each month by debiting Unearned Revenue and crediting Service Revenue ($1,200 per month if the total payment is $7,200).

6. **Bad Debt Expense:** A company estimates that a portion of its accounts receivable will not be collected. To account for this potential loss, an adjusting entry is made by debiting Bad Debt Expense and crediting Allowance for Doubtful Accounts. The amount is based on historical data or

an analysis of the collectability of accounts receivable.

These examples illustrate common types of adjusting entries made in a worksheet. The specific adjusting entries will vary depending on the nature of the business, its accounting policies, and the timing and recognition of revenues and expenses. Adjusting entries ensure that the financial statements reflect the proper recognition of revenues, expenses, assets, and liabilities in the correct accounting period.

Examples of CLOSING Entries in a Worksheet:

1. **Close Revenue Accounts:** At the end of the accounting period, the balances of revenue accounts such as Sales Revenue, Service Revenue, or Rental Income are closed. The closing entry for these accounts involves debiting the respective revenue accounts and crediting the Income Summary account. For example:
   Debit: Sales Revenue Credit: Income Summary

2. **Close Expense Accounts:** Similarly, the balances of expense accounts such as Rent Expense, Salaries Expense, or Advertising Expense are closed. The closing entry for these accounts involves debiting the Expense Summary account and crediting the respective expense accounts. For example:
   Debit: Expense Summary Credit: Rent Expense

3. **Close Income Summary Account:** After transferring the revenue and expense account

balances to the Income Summary account, the balance of the Income Summary account is closed by transferring it to the Retained Earnings or Owner's Equity account. If the Income Summary account shows a net income, the entry will be:

Debit: Income Summary Credit: Retained Earnings

If the Income Summary account shows a net loss, the entry will be the reverse:

Debit: Retained Earnings Credit: Income Summary

4. Close Dividend Accounts: If the company pays dividends to its shareholders, the Dividends account is closed. The closing entry for the Dividends account involves debiting Retained Earnings (or Owner's Equity) and crediting Dividends. For example:

Debit: Retained Earnings Credit: Dividends

These examples demonstrate the closing entries made in a worksheet. The purpose of closing entries is to reset the temporary accounts (revenue, expense, and dividend accounts) to zero at the end of the accounting period, ensuring that they are ready to record transactions in the subsequent period. By closing these accounts, the net income or net loss for the period is transferred to the Retained Earnings (or Owner's Equity) account, and the Dividends account is closed to reflect the distribution of profits to shareholders.

It's important to note that the specific accounts and amounts used in closing entries will vary depending on the business and its chart of accounts. Additionally, the closing entries are typically made after the adjusting entries and before preparing the financial statements.

CHAPTER TEN
Financial Accounting and Financial Reporting

Financial accounting and financial reporting play crucial roles in providing relevant and reliable information about a company's financial performance and position. They serve several important purposes, which can be summarized as follows:

1. **Providing Information to External Stakeholders:** Financial accounting and reporting serve as a means of communicating financial information to external stakeholders, such as investors, creditors, regulators, and the general public. These stakeholders rely on financial statements to make informed decisions about investing in or lending to a company. The purpose is to provide transparency and accountability, enabling stakeholders to assess the company's financial health, profitability, and risks.

2. **Facilitating Investment Decisions:** Financial accounting and reporting help investors assess the viability and profitability of potential investment opportunities. By examining financial statements, investors can evaluate a company's past performance, current financial position, and future prospects. This information assists in determining whether to invest in the company's stock, bonds, or other securities.

3. **Assisting Creditors and Lenders:** Financial accounting and reporting play a crucial role in enabling creditors and lenders to evaluate the creditworthiness and repayment capacity of a company. Creditors, such as banks and financial institutions, analyze financial statements to assess the risk associated with lending money to a company. They consider factors such as liquidity, solvency, and cash flow to determine the company's ability to meet its financial obligations.

4. **Meeting Regulatory Requirements:** Financial accounting and reporting are essential for complying with various regulatory frameworks and reporting standards. Companies are required to prepare and disclose financial statements in accordance with Generally Accepted Accounting Principles (GAAP) or International Financial Reporting Standards (IFRS), depending on the jurisdiction. Compliance with these standards ensures consistency and comparability in financial reporting, promoting transparency and credibility.

5. **Evaluating Management Performance:** Financial accounting and reporting assist in evaluating the performance of a company's management. By analyzing financial statements, stakeholders can assess how effectively management has utilized the company's resources and generated profits. Financial ratios and key performance indicators derived from financial statements provide insights into profitability, efficiency, and return on investment.

6. **Assessing Financial Health and Sustainability:** Financial accounting and reporting help stakeholders gauge a company's financial health and long-term sustainability. By analyzing financial statements, stakeholders can assess factors such as liquidity, solvency, and profitability. These indicators provide insights into a company's ability to meet short-term obligations, manage long-term debt, generate profits, and sustain growth.

7. **Supporting Decision-Making:** Financial accounting and reporting provide valuable information for making various business decisions. Managers use financial statements to assess the financial implications of strategic choices, investment decisions, pricing strategies, cost management, and resource allocation. The information helps in evaluating the financial impact of different alternatives and selecting the most favorable course of action.

8. **Facilitating Investor Relations:** Financial accounting and reporting contribute to building trust and maintaining positive relationships with investors and shareholders. Clear and accurate financial statements enhance investor confidence and promote transparency. Regular and reliable financial reporting fosters open communication between the company and its shareholders, facilitating engagement and long-term investment.

The purpose of financial accounting and financial reporting is to provide accurate, reliable, and relevant information about a company's financial performance and position. By doing so, they enable stakeholders to make informed decisions, evaluate the company's financial health, and assess its prospects for the future. These processes promote transparency, accountability, and trust in the business community, contributing to the overall stability and efficiency of financial markets.

A. Benefactors of Financial Reporting
Financial reporting serves the interests of various stakeholders who rely on financial information to make informed decisions. The primary beneficiaries of financial reporting include investors, creditors, lenders, regulators, employees, and management. Let's explore their roles and the timing of financial statement preparation.

1. **Investors:** Investors are one of the key beneficiaries of financial reporting. They include individuals, institutions, and shareholders who provide capital to a company in exchange for ownership or investment returns. Investors use financial statements to assess the company's financial performance, profitability, and growth potential. This information helps them make decisions about buying, holding, or selling investments.

2. **Creditors and Lenders:** Creditors and lenders, such as banks and financial institutions, rely on financial reporting to evaluate the creditworthiness and repayment capacity of a company. They analyze financial statements to assess the company's ability

to meet its financial obligations and evaluate the risk associated with lending money. This information helps creditors determine the terms and conditions for providing credit or loans to the company.

3. **Regulators and Government Authorities:** Regulators and government authorities use financial reporting to ensure compliance with accounting standards, regulations, and tax requirements. Financial statements help regulators monitor the financial health of companies, enforce legal and reporting obligations, and safeguard the interests of investors and the public. They also use financial statements for economic analysis, policy-making, and regulatory purposes.

4. **Employees:** Employees, both current and prospective, can benefit from financial reporting. Financial statements provide insights into a company's financial stability, profitability, and growth prospects. This information helps employees assess the financial health of their employer and make decisions related to compensation, job security, and career opportunities.

5. **Management:** Management uses financial reporting as a tool for decision-making, planning, and performance evaluation. Financial statements provide an overview of the company's financial performance, position, and cash flows. This information helps management evaluate business strategies, allocate resources, identify areas of

improvement, and assess the impact of decisions on the company's financial results.

B. The Four Financial Statements

The financial statements of a business are formal documents that summarize and present the financial performance and position of an organization. They provide crucial information about the company's financial activities, profitability, liquidity, and overall health. There are four main types of financial statements: the balance sheet, income statement, statement of cash flows, and statement of changes in equity.

1. **Balance Sheet:** The balance sheet, also known as the statement of financial position, provides a snapshot of a company's financial position at a specific point in time. It presents the organization's assets, liabilities, and equity. Assets represent what the company owns, including cash, accounts receivable, inventory, and property. Liabilities represent the company's obligations, such as loans, accounts payable, and accrued expenses. Equity represents the residual interest in the assets after deducting liabilities, including retained earnings and share capital. The balance sheet follows the fundamental accounting equation: Assets = Liabilities + Equity.

2. **Income Statement:** The income statement, also called the statement of comprehensive income or profit and loss statement, reports the revenues, expenses, gains, and losses of a business over a specific period. It shows the company's financial

performance by indicating whether it generated a profit or incurred a loss. The income statement starts with revenue, which is the inflow of economic benefits from the sale of goods or services. It then deducts various expenses, such as the cost of goods sold, operating expenses, interest, and taxes, to arrive at the net income or net loss.

3. **Statement of Cash Flows:** The statement of cash flows provides information about the cash inflows and outflows of a business during a particular period. It categorizes cash flows into three main activities: operating, investing, and financing. Operating activities include cash transactions related to the company's primary operations, such as sales, payments to suppliers, and employee salaries. Investing activities involve cash flows from the buying or selling of long-term assets, such as property, plant, and equipment. Financing activities include cash flows from activities such as issuing or repaying debt, issuing or repurchasing shares, and paying dividends.

4. **Statement of Changes in Equity:** The statement of changes in equity, also known as the statement of retained earnings, shows how the equity of a company has changed over a specific period. It presents the beginning balance of equity, adjustments for net income or loss, additional investments or withdrawals by owners, dividends paid, and other changes in equity. The statement provides insights into the factors that contributed to changes in the company's equity position.

These financial statements are prepared in accordance with accounting principles and standards, such as GAAP or IFRS, to ensure consistency and comparability across different companies. They are important tools for external users, such as investors, creditors, and regulatory authorities, to assess the financial health, performance, and stability of a business. Internally, financial statements help management analyze and evaluate the company's financial performance, make informed decisions, and develop strategies for growth and profitability.

C. Financial Statements and Company's Performance

Financial statements are comprehensive reports that provide a snapshot of a company's financial performance and position. They are vital tools used by businesses, investors, lenders, and other stakeholders to assess the financial health and make informed decisions. This book will examine the details of financial statements, including their structure, the accounts included on each statement, their importance, the users of financial statements, and the significance of certification.

I. Overview of Financial Statements:

Financial statements consist of four key reports:

1. **Balance Sheet:** The balance sheet presents the financial position of a company at a specific point in time. It includes assets, liabilities, and shareholders' equity. Assets represent what the company owns, liabilities indicate what the company owes, and

shareholders' equity shows the owners' stake in the company.

2. **Income Statement:** The income statement, also known as the profit and loss statement, showcases a company's revenues, expenses, and net income over a specific period. It provides insights into the company's operational performance, profitability, and ability to generate profits.

3. **Statement of Cash Flows:** The statement of cash flows outlines the cash inflows and outflows of a company during a specific period. It categorizes cash flows into operating activities, investing activities, and financing activities. This statement reveals the company's ability to generate and manage cash.

4. **Statement of Shareholders' Equity:** The statement of shareholders' equity reflects the changes in the shareholders' equity accounts over a given period. It includes items such as issued capital, retained earnings, and other comprehensive income. This statement shows how the company's equity position has changed due to net income, dividends, and other transactions.

II. Accounts on Each Financial Statement:

1. Balance Sheet Accounts:

- Assets: Cash, accounts receivable, inventory, property, plant, and equipment, investments, and intangible assets.

- Liabilities: Accounts payable, loans payable, accrued expenses, deferred revenues, and long-term debt.
- Shareholders' Equity: Common stock, preferred stock, retained earnings, and additional paid-in capital.

2. Income Statement Accounts:

- Revenues: Sales revenue, service revenue, rental income, and other operating revenues.
- Expenses: Cost of goods sold, salaries and wages, rent, utilities, depreciation, and interest expenses.

3. Statement of Cash Flows Accounts:

- Operating Activities: Cash received from customers, cash paid to suppliers, and cash paid for operating expenses.
- Investing Activities: Cash inflows and outflows from buying or selling long-term assets or investments.
- Financing Activities: Cash inflows and outflows from borrowing or repaying loans, issuing or repurchasing stock, and paying dividends.
4. Statement of Shareholders' Equity Accounts:
- Issued Capital: Common stock, preferred stock, and additional paid-in capital.
- Retained Earnings: Accumulated profits or losses from prior periods.

- Other Comprehensive Income: Gains or losses from foreign currency translation, pension adjustments, or unrealized gains or losses on investments.

III. Importance of Financial Statements:

1. **Performance Evaluation:** Financial statements allow stakeholders to evaluate a company's financial performance, profitability, and growth over time. They help assess the company's ability to generate profits, manage expenses, and utilize assets efficiently.

2. **Decision-Making:** Financial statements provide critical information for making informed decisions. Investors use them to evaluate investment opportunities, lenders assess creditworthiness, and management relies on them for strategic planning and resource allocation.

3. **Transparency and Accountability:** Financial statements promote transparency and accountability by providing a clear overview of a company's financial activities. They help maintain ethical standards, comply with regulations, and promote trust among stakeholders.

4. **Financial Health Assessment:** Financial statements aid in assessing a company's financial health, including liquidity, solvency, and profitability. They provide insights into the company's ability to meet

211

short-term obligations, pay long-term debts, and generate sustainable profits.

5. **Comparability and Benchmarking:** Financial statements enable stakeholders to compare a company's performance with industry peers, competitors, or prior periods. They serve as benchmarks for measuring a company's financial position, performance, and growth.

IV. Users of Financial Statements:

1. **Investors and Shareholders:** Investors and shareholders analyze financial statements to make investment decisions, assess the value of their investments, and evaluate dividend potential.

2. **Lenders and Creditors:** Lenders and creditors rely on financial statements to evaluate a company's creditworthiness, determine borrowing capacity, and assess the risk of lending.

3. **Management and Board of Directors:** Management and board members utilize financial statements to evaluate the company's financial performance, set strategic goals, and make informed business decisions.

4. **Government Agencies and Tax Authorities:** Government agencies and tax authorities use financial statements to ensure compliance with regulations, assess tax liabilities, and monitor financial activities.

5. **Analysts and Financial Advisors:** Financial analysts and advisors analyze financial statements to provide insights, forecasts, and recommendations to clients, investors, or management.

V. Certification of Financial Statements:

Financial statements are typically certified by an external auditor or a certified public accountant (CPA). Certification involves an independent review and verification of the financial statements' accuracy, adherence to accounting principles, and compliance with relevant regulations. Certification provides assurance to stakeholders that the financial statements are reliable, credible, and fairly represent the company's financial position and performance.

Financial statements play a pivotal role in assessing a company's financial health, facilitating decision-making, and promoting transparency. They provide a comprehensive view of a company's financial activities, performance, and position. Various stakeholders rely on financial statements to make investment decisions, evaluate creditworthiness, and monitor financial activities. Certification by external auditors or CPAs ensures the reliability and accuracy of financial statements. Understanding financial statements and their significance is crucial for effective financial management, informed decision-making, and maintaining stakeholder confidence.

Preparing financial statements involves several steps in financial accounting:

1. **Prepare the Trial Balance:** The first step is to prepare a trial balance, which lists all the accounts and their balances (debit or credit) at a specific date. The trial balance serves as a starting point for preparing the financial statements.

2. **Adjusting Entries:** Make any necessary adjusting entries to ensure that revenues, expenses, assets, and liabilities are properly recognized in the appropriate accounting period. Adjusting entries are made to account for accruals, deferrals, depreciation, and other adjustments required by the matching principle and accrual accounting.

3. **Prepare the Income Statement:** The income statement reports the revenues, expenses, gains, and losses incurred by a business over a specific period. It shows the net income or net loss of the company. To prepare the income statement, revenue accounts are listed first, followed by the expense accounts. The difference between total revenues and total expenses represents the net income or net loss.

4. **Prepare the Statement of Retained Earnings/Owner's Equity:** The statement of retained earnings (for corporations) or statement of owner's equity (for sole proprietorships and partnerships) shows the changes in the retained earnings or owner's equity account over a specific

period. It includes net income or net loss, dividends or withdrawals, and any additional capital contributions.

5. **Prepare the Balance Sheet:** The balance sheet provides a snapshot of a company's financial position at a specific point in time. It presents the assets, liabilities, and owner's equity. Assets are listed first, followed by liabilities and then owner's equity. The balance sheet follows the accounting equation: Assets = Liabilities + Owner's Equity.

6. **Prepare the Statement of Cash Flows:** The statement of cash flows shows the inflows and outflows of cash during a specific period. It is divided into three main sections: operating activities, investing activities, and financing activities. The statement of cash flows reconciles the net income from the income statement with the changes in cash and cash equivalents on the balance sheet.

7. **Analyze and Review the Financial Statements:** Once the financial statements are prepared, they should be carefully analyzed and reviewed to ensure accuracy, consistency, and compliance with accounting standards. Financial ratios and other financial analysis techniques can be used to assess the financial health and performance of the company.

8. **Disclose Additional Notes:** Financial statements are typically accompanied by footnotes or disclosures that provide additional information about significant accounting policies, contingencies, contractual

obligations, and other relevant details. These disclosures help provide a comprehensive understanding of the financial statements.

9. **Finalize and Distribute the Financial Statements:** After reviewing the financial statements and making any necessary adjustments, the final versions are prepared. The financial statements are then distributed to internal stakeholders (management, board of directors) and external parties such as investors, creditors, and regulatory authorities.

It's important to note that the specific steps involved in preparing financial statements may vary depending on the reporting requirements and accounting standards applicable to a particular entity. Additionally, professional judgment, adherence to accounting principles, and attention to detail are crucial throughout the process to ensure the accuracy and reliability of the financial statements.

CHAPTER ELEVEN
The Relationship Between the Financial Statements

he relationship between financial statements is crucial for understanding the financial health and performance of a business. The three primary financial statements— the income statement, balance sheet, and cash flow statement— are interconnected and provide valuable insights into the company's operations, profitability, liquidity, and overall financial position. By analyzing the relationships between these statements, stakeholders can make informed decisions and assess the company's financial viability. In this article, we will delve deeper into the relationship between the financial statements and explore how they complement each other.

Let's start by examining the relationship between the income statement and the balance sheet. The income statement, also known as the profit and loss statement, provides information about a company's revenue, expenses, and net income over a specific period. It highlights the company's profitability by revealing whether it generated a profit or incurred a loss. The net income figure from the income statement is then transferred to the balance sheet, specifically to the shareholder's equity section, where it is recorded as retained earnings. Retained earnings represent the accumulated profits of the company that have not been distributed to shareholders as dividends. Therefore, the income statement directly impacts the balance sheet by influencing the company's retained earnings, which is an essential component of shareholders' equity.

The balance sheet provides a snapshot of a company's financial position at a specific point in time. It consists of three main sections: assets, liabilities, and shareholders' equity. The relationship between the balance sheet and income statement is evident in how certain items from the income statement flow into the balance sheet. For example, the net income from the income statement increases retained earnings, which, in turn, increases shareholders' equity on the balance sheet. Additionally, the balance sheet includes various asset and liability accounts that are affected by the income statement. For instance, if a company generates higher net income, it may have more cash available, leading to an increase in the cash and cash equivalents reported on the balance sheet.

Moving on to the relationship between the income statement and the cash flow statement, it's important to note that the income statement focuses on accrual accounting, while the cash flow statement highlights the company's cash inflows and outflows. While the income statement provides information about revenues earned and expenses incurred, the cash flow statement provides insights into how cash moves in and out of the company. Despite their differences, these two statements are interrelated. The net income reported on the income statement serves as the starting point for preparing the cash flow statement. It is adjusted for non-cash items, such as depreciation and changes in working capital, to derive the operating cash flow. Understanding the relationship between the income statement and the cash flow statement is crucial because a company can generate significant net income but still face cash flow problems if the cash collections from customers are delayed or if there is excessive cash tied up in inventory or accounts receivable.

Furthermore, the cash flow statement also relates to the balance sheet. The ending cash balance reported on the cash flow statement is reconciled with the cash and cash equivalents reported on the balance sheet. Any changes in cash and cash equivalents during the period will affect the cash balance reported on the balance sheet. Additionally, the cash flow statement provides insights into how the company financed its operations and investments, which is crucial for assessing the company's liquidity and solvency.

The relationship between the financial statements is essential for gaining a comprehensive understanding of a company's financial performance, position, and cash flows. The income statement, balance sheet, and cash flow statement complement each other by providing different perspectives on a company's operations and financial health. Analyzing the relationships between these statements allows stakeholders to evaluate a company's profitability, liquidity, and overall financial viability. By understanding how changes in one statement impact the others, investors, creditors, and other stakeholders can make more informed decisions and assess the company's ability to generate sustainable profits and cash flows.

To provide a comprehensive understanding of financial statements and how they connect with each other, let's explore each financial statement, the sub-accounts included, and their interrelationships.

I. **Balance Sheet:** The balance sheet presents the financial position of a company at a specific point in time. It consists of the following sub-accounts:

1. **Assets:**
   - Current Assets: Cash, accounts receivable, inventory, prepaid expenses, and short-term investments.
   - Fixed Assets: Property, plant, and equipment (PP&E), including land, buildings, machinery, and vehicles.
   - Intangible Assets: Intellectual property, patents, trademarks, copyrights, and goodwill.
   - Other Assets: Long-term investments, deferred tax assets, and miscellaneous assets.

2. **Liabilities:**
   - Current Liabilities: Accounts payable, accrued expenses, short-term loans, and current portion of long-term debt.
   - Long-term Liabilities: Long-term debt, mortgages, and other long-term obligations.
   - Other Liabilities: Deferred tax liabilities, pension obligations, and miscellaneous long-term liabilities.

3. **Shareholders' Equity:**
   - Common Stock: The par value of shares issued to shareholders.
   - Additional Paid-in Capital: The amount received from shareholders above the par value.
   - Retained Earnings: Accumulated profits or losses retained in the business.
   - Treasury Stock: The cost of shares repurchased by the company.

- Other Comprehensive Income: Gains or losses that bypass the income statement, such as foreign currency translation adjustments.

The balance sheet follows the accounting equation: Assets = Liabilities + Shareholders' Equity. It demonstrates the company's financial position by showing the total value of assets financed by liabilities and shareholders' equity.

II. Income Statement: The income statement summarizes a company's revenues, expenses, gains, and losses over a specific period. It includes the following sub-accounts:

1. Revenues:
   - Sales Revenue: Revenue generated from the sale of goods or services.
   - Service Revenue: Revenue generated from providing services.
   - Other Operating Revenues: Revenue from non-primary business activities.

2. Cost of Goods Sold (COGS):
   - Direct Costs: Costs directly associated with producing or acquiring goods.
   - Indirect Costs: Overhead costs allocated to production.

3. Operating Expenses:
   - Selling Expenses: Costs related to selling products or services.
   - Administrative Expenses: Costs associated with general management and administration.

- Research and Development Expenses: Costs incurred in developing new products or processes.
- Depreciation and Amortization: The systematic allocation of the cost of assets over their useful lives.

4. Other Income and Expenses:
   - Interest Income and Expenses: Income earned from investments and expenses related to borrowing.
   - Gain/Loss on Sale of Assets: Profit or loss from the sale of non-inventory assets.
   - Income Tax Expense: Taxes owed based on taxable income.

The income statement shows the company's revenue generation, cost structure, and overall profitability. Net Income (Revenues - Expenses) flows from the income statement to the statement of retained earnings.

III. **Statement of Retained Earnings:** The statement of retained earnings reconciles the beginning and ending balances of retained earnings during a period. It includes the following sub-accounts:

1. Beginning Retained Earnings: The balance of retained earnings at the beginning of the period.
2. Net Income: The net profit or loss from the income statement.
3. Dividends: The portion of profits distributed to shareholders as dividends.

4. Other Adjustments: Any other changes to retained earnings, such as corrections or prior-period adjustments.

The ending balance of retained earnings from this statement flows to the balance sheet's shareholders' equity section.

IV. Statement of Cash Flows: The statement of cash flows summarizes a company's cash inflows and outflows during a specific period. It consists of the following sub-accounts:

1. Operating Activities:
   - Cash received from customers for sales or services.
   - Cash paid to suppliers for inventory and operating expenses.
   - Cash paid for income taxes and interest expenses.

2. Investing Activities:
   - Cash used for the acquisition or sale of long-term assets.
   - Cash received from the sale of long-term assets or investments.

3. Financing Activities:
   - Cash received from issuing stocks or borrowing.
   - Cash paid for dividends, debt repayments, or share repurchases.

The statement of cash flows reconciles the changes in the company's cash position, highlighting its ability to generate and manage cash.

Interconnections between Financial Statements: Financial statements are interconnected and rely on each other to provide a comprehensive view of a company's financial performance and position.

- Net Income from the income statement flows to the statement of retained earnings, increasing or decreasing the retained earnings balance.
- The ending balance of retained earnings from the statement of retained earnings is reported on the balance sheet's shareholders' equity section.
- The cash balance from the statement of cash flows is reported on the balance sheet's cash and cash equivalents line item.
- Changes in the balance sheet accounts, such as investments, loans, or property purchases, are reflected in the statement of cash flows under investing and financing activities.
- The balance sheet's ending balances are carried forward as the beginning balances for the next accounting period.

Financial statements are crucial tools for understanding a company's financial health, performance, and position. Each statement serves a specific purpose, with sub-accounts providing detailed information about various aspects of the business. The interconnectedness of financial statements ensures consistency and accuracy in reporting.

CHAPTER TWELVE
Reconciling Bank Statements

Reconciling bank statements is a crucial financial practice that ensures the accuracy and integrity of a company's financial records. It involves comparing the transactions recorded in the company's books with the transactions reported by the bank in its statement. The process of reconciling bank statements helps identify discrepancies, errors, or fraudulent activities, thereby providing a clear and accurate picture of the company's cash position. In this article, we will delve deeper into the process of reconciling bank statements and discuss its importance for businesses.

The first step in reconciling bank statements is to obtain the bank statement for the relevant period, which typically covers a month. This statement provides a detailed record of all transactions that occurred in the company's bank account during that period. These transactions include deposits, withdrawals, checks cleared, electronic transfers, fees, and any other activity related to the account. The company needs to compare the transactions listed in its own accounting records, often referred to as the cash book or general ledger, with the transactions reported in the bank statement. This comparison is typically done line by line, ensuring that each transaction is accounted for and properly recorded in both sets of records.

During the reconciliation process, several factors can cause discrepancies between the company's records and the bank statement. These factors include timing differences, errors, outstanding checks, deposits in transit, bank fees, and interest earned or charged. Let's explore each of these factors in more detail:

1. **Timing differences:** Transactions may appear in the company's books in a different period than when they are recorded by the bank. For example, a check issued by the company at the end of the month may not clear the bank until the beginning of the following month, resulting in a timing difference.

2. **Errors:** Errors can occur in both the company's records and the bank's statement. These errors may include incorrectly recorded amounts, transposition errors, or duplicate entries. It's important to thoroughly review both sets of records to identify and correct any such errors.

3. **Outstanding checks:** Outstanding checks are checks that have been issued by the company but have not yet been presented to the bank for payment. These checks need to be deducted from the company's cash balance in the bank statement as they have not yet reduced the company's actual cash position.

4. **Deposits in transit:** Deposits in transit are cash or check deposits made by the company that have not yet been credited to the bank account. These deposits need to be added to the company's cash balance in the bank statement as they increase the company's actual cash position.

5. **Bank fees:** Banks often charge various fees for services provided, such as monthly maintenance

fees, transaction fees, or wire transfer fees. These fees need to be accounted for and deducted from the company's cash balance in the bank statement.

6. **Interest earned or charged:** If the company's bank account earns interest or incurs interest charges, these amounts need to be reconciled between the company's records and the bank statement.

To reconcile the bank statement effectively, the company needs to make necessary adjustments to its own records to account for the factors mentioned above. This may involve updating the cash book or general ledger to reflect the correct balances and properly record any outstanding checks, deposits in transit, bank fees, or interest earned or charged. The ultimate goal of reconciling bank statements is to ensure that the ending balance of the bank statement matches the company's adjusted cash balance as per its own records. When these balances align, it indicates that all transactions have been properly recorded and accounted for, and the company's financial records are accurate.

The importance of reconciling bank statements cannot be overstated. It serves as a critical control mechanism for detecting errors, omissions, or fraudulent activities. Reconciling bank statements regularly helps uncover any discrepancies at an early stage, allowing for timely resolution and preventing potential financial losses or misstatements in the company's financial statements. Moreover, reconciling bank statements provides assurance to internal and external stakeholders regarding the company's financial integrity and reliability. Investors, creditors, and auditors often rely on accurate financial records to make informed decisions or to conduct audits. By regularly reconciling bank statements, the company demonstrates its commitment to maintaining accurate financial records and strengthens stakeholder confidence in its financial reporting.

Reconciling bank statements is an essential financial practice that ensures the accuracy and integrity of a company's financial records. It involves comparing the transactions recorded in the company's books with those reported in the bank statement and making necessary adjustments to account for discrepancies. Regular reconciliation helps identify errors, outstanding checks, deposits in transit, bank fees, and interest, providing a clear and accurate picture of the company's cash position. By reconciling bank statements, businesses can maintain reliable financial records, detect errors or fraudulent activities, and build trust among stakeholders.

Reconciling bank statements each month is an important practice in financial accounting and has several key purposes. Here are the main reasons why bank statement reconciliation is necessary:

1. **Accuracy Verification:** Reconciling bank statements helps verify the accuracy of both the company's records and the bank's records. By comparing the company's internal records of transactions with the information provided on the bank statement, any discrepancies or errors can be identified and resolved promptly. This process ensures that the financial records of the company are correct and complete.

2. **Detection of Errors or Fraud:** Bank statement reconciliation serves as a means to detect errors or potentially fraudulent activities. Discrepancies between the company's records and the bank statement, such as unauthorized transactions or discrepancies in amounts, can signal potential issues. By reconciling the bank statement, such discrepancies can be investigated and resolved in a timely manner, reducing the risk of financial loss or fraudulent activities.

3. **Cash Flow Monitoring:** Reconciling bank statements allows for the monitoring of cash flow within the company. By comparing the company's cash account balance to the bank statement's ending cash balance, any discrepancies can be identified and investigated. This process helps ensure that the company's cash inflows and outflows are accurately recorded and that the company has a clear understanding of its available cash position.

4. **Timely Identification of Bank Errors:** Banks can occasionally make errors in processing transactions or recording them on the bank statement. By regularly reconciling the bank statement, any discrepancies caused by bank errors can be identified and promptly resolved. This prevents potential issues such as incorrect charges, duplicate transactions, or missing deposits from going unnoticed, which can impact the company's financial records and cash flow.

5. **Fraud Prevention and Internal Controls:** Regular bank statement reconciliation serves as an important internal control measure to detect and prevent fraudulent activities. It helps identify unauthorized transactions, forged checks, or suspicious activities that may require further investigation. By promptly identifying and addressing such issues, companies can strengthen their internal controls and mitigate the risk of financial fraud.

6. **Financial Statement Accuracy:** Bank balances are often a significant component of a company's financial statements, such as the balance sheet or cash flow statement. Reconciling bank statements ensures that the cash and bank account balances reported in the financial statements accurately reflect the actual financial position of the company. This enhances the reliability and credibility of the financial statements for internal decision-making, external stakeholders, and regulatory compliance.

Reconciling bank statements each month is a critical financial practice that helps verify the accuracy of financial records, detect errors or fraudulent activities, monitor cash flow, and strengthen internal controls. It promotes financial transparency, ensures the reliability of financial statements, and contributes to sound financial management within the company.

Examples of Bank Reconciliation:

Example 1: Deposits in Transit and Outstanding Checks
Bank Statement:

- Ending balance per bank statement: $10,000
- Deposits in transit: $2,000
- Outstanding checks: $1,500

Company's Books:

- Ending balance per company's records: $9,000
- Deposits in transit: $2,000
- Outstanding checks: $1,500

Bank Reconciliation:

- Add deposits in transit: $2,000
- Deduct outstanding checks: $1,500

Adjusted Bank Balance: $10,500 Adjusted Book Balance: $10,500

Example 2: Bank Errors and Service Charges Bank Statement:

- Ending balance per bank statement: $7,500
- Bank error: Overstatement of $500
- Bank service charge: $50

Company's Books:

- Ending balance per company's records: $7,000

Bank Reconciliation:

- Deduct bank error: $500
- Deduct bank service charge: $50

Adjusted Bank Balance: $6,950 Adjusted Book Balance: $7,000

Example 3: NSF (Non-Sufficient Funds) Check and Interest Earned Bank Statement:

- Ending balance per bank statement: $15,000
- NSF check returned: $1,000
- Interest earned: $200

Company's Books:

- Ending balance per company's records: $15,200

Bank Reconciliation:

- Deduct NSF check: $1,000
- Add interest earned: $200

Adjusted Bank Balance: $14,200 Adjusted Book Balance: $14,200

In these examples, the bank reconciliation process involves comparing the bank statement with the company's records to identify any differences. Deposits in transit, outstanding checks, bank errors, service charges, NSF checks, and interest earned are considered to reconcile the balances. By making necessary adjustments to the bank and book balances, the reconciled balances are obtained, ensuring that the company's financial records and the bank statement align.

It's important to note that the specific items and amounts in bank reconciliation will vary depending on the transactions and circumstances of each company. The reconciliation process aims to identify and resolve discrepancies to ensure the accuracy of financial records and maintain the integrity of the company's financial position.

CHAPTER THIRTEEN
Performing Accounts Payables Functions

The accounts payable process is an essential component of the financial operations of a company. It involves the management and tracking of payments owed to suppliers, vendors, and other creditors. This process ensures that invoices and bills are processed accurately, timely payments are made, and the company maintains strong relationships with its business partners. Here, we will examine the details of the accounts payable process, including the steps involved and provide a flowchart to illustrate the process visually.

The Accounts Payable Process:

1. **Invoice Receipt:** The process begins with the receipt of invoices from suppliers or vendors. Invoices can be received in various formats, including paper-based invoices, electronic invoices, or through online portals. Upon receipt, the invoices are reviewed to ensure they are complete and accurate. They typically include details such as the supplier's name, invoice number, description of the goods or services, quantity, unit price, total amount due, and payment terms.

2. **Invoice Verification and Approval:** Once the invoices are received, they undergo a verification and approval process. This involves verifying the accuracy and validity of the invoices by matching them against purchase orders, receiving reports, and other supporting documents. The invoices are

reviewed for pricing accuracy, quantity received, and any discrepancies. They are then approved by authorized personnel, such as department managers or designated individuals responsible for approving payments.

3. **Purchase Order Matching:** If a purchase order exists for the goods or services being invoiced, the accounts payable team matches the invoice against the purchase order and receiving report. This step ensures that the items or services were indeed ordered and received by the company. Any discrepancies or differences between the invoice and purchase order are investigated and resolved before proceeding.

4. **Recording in the Accounting System:** Once the invoices are verified and approved, they are recorded in the company's accounting system. The accounts payable team enters the invoice details, including the supplier's name, invoice number, date, amount, and other relevant information, into the accounting software or ERP system. This step creates a record of the liability owed to the supplier and updates the accounts payable ledger.

5. **Payment Processing:** After the invoices are recorded, the payment processing phase begins. The accounts payable team prepares payment batches based on the payment terms and schedules. Payment methods can include checks, electronic funds transfers (EFT), or other electronic payment systems. The payment batches are reviewed and approved by

authorized personnel, and the payments are scheduled for release.

6. **Cash Management:** As payments are released, the accounts payable team coordinates with the cash management or treasury department to ensure sufficient funds are available to cover the payments. Cash flow projections and forecasting play a crucial role in managing payment schedules and maintaining good relationships with suppliers.

7. **Reconciliation and Reporting:** Once payments are made, the accounts payable team reconciles the payments with the corresponding invoices in the accounting system. This reconciliation process helps identify any discrepancies or outstanding payments that need to be addressed. The team also generates reports summarizing the accounts payable activity, such as aging reports, vendor payment history, and cash flow analysis.

8. **Vendor Relationship Management:** Throughout the accounts payable process, maintaining positive relationships with vendors and suppliers is crucial. Timely payments, prompt communication, and addressing any concerns or disputes contribute to strong vendor relationships. The accounts payable team often interacts with vendors to resolve payment inquiries, address discrepancies, and ensure a smooth payment process.

Flowchart of the Accounts Payable Process:

[Start] --> [Invoice Receipt] --> [Invoice Verification and Approval] --> [Purchase Order Matching] --> [Recording in Accounting System] --> [Payment Processing] --> [Cash Management] --> [Reconciliation and Reporting] --> [Vendor Relationship Management] --> [End]

The flowchart illustrates the sequential steps involved in the accounts payable process. It begins with the receipt of invoices and progresses through verification, matching, recording, payment processing, cash management, reconciliation, reporting, and vendor relationship management. The flowchart provides a visual representation of the accounts payable process, highlighting the interdependencies and progression of activities.

The accounts payable process is a critical aspect of managing a company's financial obligations to suppliers and vendors. It involves several steps, including invoice receipt, verification, approval, purchase order matching, recording in the accounting system, payment processing, cash management, reconciliation, reporting, and vendor relationship management. Following a well-defined accounts payable process helps ensure accuracy, efficiency, and compliance in managing and paying the company's liabilities, while also fostering strong business relationships with suppliers and vendors.

Accounts Payable (AP) is a vital function within an organization's finance department that deals with managing and processing the company's outstanding payments to vendors, suppliers, and creditors. A career in accounts payable involves handling financial transactions, ensuring accuracy and timeliness in payment processing, and maintaining strong vendor relationships. In this article, we will explore the field of accounts payable, discuss the typical processes involved, and highlight the career opportunities it offers.

Accounts Payables Careers

A career in accounts payable offers several opportunities for professional growth and development. Here are some potential roles within the field:

1. **Accounts Payable Clerk:** This entry-level position involves the day-to-day processing of invoices and payments. Accounts payable clerks typically handle data entry, invoice verification, and payment processing tasks under the supervision of more senior professionals.

2. **Accounts Payable Specialist:** As professionals gain experience and expertise, they can progress to the role of an accounts payable specialist. Specialists take on more complex tasks such as resolving invoice discrepancies, managing vendor relationships, and ensuring compliance with accounting standards and regulations.

3. **Accounts Payable Supervisor/Manager:** In this leadership role, individuals oversee the accounts payable team, manage departmental workflows, and ensure that all payments are processed accurately and in a timely manner. They may also implement

process improvements, develop policies and procedures, and provide training to team members.

4. **Financial Analyst:** With a solid foundation in accounts payable, professionals can transition into financial analyst roles where they contribute to financial planning, budgeting, and forecasting activities. Financial analysts analyze financial data, identify trends, and provide insights to support strategic decision-making.

To excel in an accounts payable career, certain skills and qualities are essential:

1. **Attention to detail:** Accounts payable professionals must possess strong attention to detail to accurately process and reconcile invoices and payments. Even minor errors can have significant financial implications.

2. **Analytical skills:** The ability to analyze and interpret financial data is crucial for identifying discrepancies, detecting fraudulent activities, and providing insights to improve processes.

3. **Communication skills:** Effective communication is vital when interacting with vendors, colleagues, and other stakeholders. Accounts payable professionals need to articulate payment status, address inquiries, and negotiate favorable terms with vendors.

4. **Organizational skills:** Accounts payable professionals often handle multiple invoices and payments simultaneously. Strong organizational skills help ensure that deadlines are met and payments are processed efficiently.

5. **Technological proficiency:** Proficiency in accounting software and other relevant tools is essential for efficient invoice processing, payment initiation, and data analysis.

A career in accounts payable involves managing and processing payments owed by a company to vendors and suppliers. Accounts payable professionals play a crucial role in maintaining accurate financial records, ensuring timely payment processing, and building strong vendor relationships. The field offers opportunities for growth, from entry-level positions to leadership roles.

CHAPTER FOURTEEN
Performing Accounts Receivables Functions

The accounts receivable process is a fundamental component of a company's financial operations. It involves managing and tracking payments owed to the company by its customers or clients. The accounts receivable process ensures that invoices are issued accurately, payments are received promptly, and customer relationships are maintained. In this detailed explanation, we will explore the various steps involved in the accounts receivable process and provide a flowchart to visualize the process.

The Accounts Receivable Process:

1. **Sales and Invoicing:** The process begins with the sale of goods or services to customers. Once the sale is completed, an invoice is generated, detailing the transaction's key information. This includes the customer's name, invoice number, date, description of the goods or services, quantity, unit price, total amount due, and payment terms.

2. **Invoice Delivery:** After the invoice is generated, it is sent to the customer. This can be done through various means, such as email, mail, or electronic invoicing systems. It is important to ensure that the invoice is delivered to the correct recipient and that the customer has received it.

3. **Invoice Validation and Approval:** Upon receiving the invoice, the customer reviews it for accuracy and

completeness. They verify that the goods or services were received as expected and that there are no discrepancies. If any issues are identified, the customer may raise queries or request adjustments. Once the invoice is validated, the customer approves it for payment.

4. **Recording in the Accounting System:** Upon receiving approval from the customer, the accounts receivable team records the invoice in the company's accounting system. This step involves entering the invoice details, including the customer's name, invoice number, date, amount, and other relevant information. The invoice is then added to the accounts receivable ledger, creating a record of the amount owed by the customer.

5. **Payment Collection:** After the invoice is recorded, the company initiates the payment collection process. This may involve sending reminders or statements to customers regarding their outstanding balances. Depending on the agreed-upon payment terms, customers may have a specific period to remit payment. The company may provide various payment options, such as checks, bank transfers, credit cards, or online payment platforms, to facilitate timely and convenient payments.

6. **Cash Application:** Once the customer's payment is received, the accounts receivable team applies the payment to the appropriate invoice in the accounting system. This ensures accurate tracking of payments and reduces outstanding balances. The team verifies

that the payment amount matches the invoiced amount and updates the accounts receivable ledger accordingly.

7. **Account Reconciliation:** Periodically, the accounts receivable team reconciles customer accounts to ensure accuracy and identify any discrepancies. This involves comparing the outstanding balances in the accounts receivable ledger with the customer's records and resolving any discrepancies or disputes. Reconciliation helps maintain accurate and up-to-date customer account information.

8. **Aging Analysis:** An aging analysis is conducted to monitor the aging of accounts receivable balances. It categorizes outstanding invoices based on their due dates, allowing the company to identify any overdue or delinquent accounts. Aging analysis provides valuable insights into the company's cash flow, collection efficiency, and potential credit risks.

9. **Collection Efforts:** For overdue or delinquent accounts, the accounts receivable team initiates collection efforts. This can involve sending reminder notices, making collection calls, or engaging collection agencies or legal processes if necessary. The goal is to minimize the time it takes to collect outstanding payments and reduce bad debts.

10. **Reporting and Analysis:** The accounts receivable process generates various reports and analysis to assess the company's receivables performance. This includes reports on outstanding balances, aging

reports, collection trends, and customer creditworthiness. These reports help identify areas for improvement, monitor cash flow, and support decision-making.

Flowchart of the Accounts Receivable Process:

[Start] --> [Sales and Invoicing] --> [Invoice Delivery] --> [Invoice Validation and Approval] --> [Recording in Accounting System] --> [Payment Collection] --> [Cash Application] --> [Account Reconciliation] --> [Aging Analysis] --> [Collection Efforts] --> [Reporting and Analysis] --> [End]

The flowchart provides a visual representation of the sequential steps involved in the accounts receivable process. It outlines the progression from sales and invoicing to invoice delivery, validation, recording, payment collection, cash application, account reconciliation, aging analysis, collection efforts, and reporting.

The accounts receivable process plays a crucial role in managing and tracking customer payments. It encompasses activities such as sales and invoicing, invoice delivery, validation and approval, recording in the accounting system, payment collection, cash application, account reconciliation, aging analysis, collection efforts, and reporting. Following a well-defined accounts receivable process ensures accurate record-keeping, timely payment collection, effective customer relationship management, and informed decision-making.

Accounts Payable and Accounts Receivable Interrelations

The accounts payable and accounts receivable processes are interrelated and interconnected between companies, forming a financial flow that impacts the overall business transactions. Understanding how these processes connect is crucial for maintaining healthy financial relationships with suppliers and customers. In this detailed explanation, we will explore the connection and flow between accounts payables and accounts receivables processes.

Accounts Payable Process

The accounts payable process involves managing and tracking payments owed by a company to its suppliers or vendors. When a company purchases goods or services on credit, it incurs an accounts payable liability. The process begins with the receipt of invoices from suppliers, which are reviewed, verified, and approved. The invoices are then recorded in the accounting system, and payments are processed. The accounts payable process ensures accurate recording, timely payments, and strong vendor relationships.

Accounts Receivable Process

On the other hand, the accounts receivable process involves managing and tracking payments owed to a company by its customers or clients. When a company sells goods or services on credit, it creates an accounts receivable asset. The process starts with generating and delivering invoices to customers, who validate and approve them. The invoices are then recorded in the accounting system, and payments are collected. The accounts receivable process ensures accurate tracking, timely collection, and customer relationship management.

Connection between Accounts Payable and Accounts Receivable: The connection between accounts payable and accounts receivable lies in the interaction between companies as suppliers and customers. Let's explore how the flow between these processes takes place:

1. **Purchase Orders and Sales Orders:** The accounts payable process is initiated when a company places a purchase order with a supplier to procure goods or services. Simultaneously, the accounts receivable process is triggered when a company receives a sales order from a customer. These orders serve as the basis for future transactions and set the foundation for accounts payable and accounts receivable activities.

2. **Invoicing:** Once the goods or services are delivered, the supplier generates an invoice and sends it to the customer. This invoice captures the details of the transaction, including the quantity, price, and terms of payment. The customer verifies the invoice and validates it for payment.

3. **Recording in Accounting Systems:** Both the accounts payable and accounts receivable teams record the invoices in their respective accounting systems. In the accounts payable process, the invoice is recorded as a liability owed to the supplier. In the accounts receivable process, the invoice is recorded

as an asset representing the amount owed by the customer.

4. **Payment Processing:** In the accounts payable process, the company reviews and approves the invoices received from suppliers and proceeds to process the payments. Payment methods can include checks, electronic fund transfers, or other electronic payment systems. The accounts receivable process involves the company sending invoices to customers and collecting payments based on the agreed-upon terms. Payment collection methods may vary, such as checks, bank transfers, credit cards, or online payment platforms.

5. **Cash Flow Impact:** The payment made by the company in the accounts payable process reduces the accounts payable liability and impacts the company's cash flow. On the other hand, the payment received by the company in the accounts receivable process increases cash flow and reduces the accounts receivable asset.

6. **Reconciliation:** Both the accounts payable and accounts receivable teams reconcile their respective records periodically. In accounts payable, reconciliation ensures that the payments made match the recorded liabilities, and any discrepancies are addressed. In accounts receivable, reconciliation verifies that the payments received align with the recorded assets, and any discrepancies or outstanding balances are resolved.

7. **Reporting and Financial Statements:** The accounts payable and accounts receivable processes generate reports and contribute to the preparation of financial statements. Accounts payable reports provide insights into outstanding liabilities, payment trends, and vendor management. Accounts receivable reports track outstanding receivables, collection efforts, aging analysis, and customer creditworthiness. These reports are crucial for financial analysis, decision-making, and assessing the overall financial health of the company.

8. **Relationship Management:** The accounts payable and accounts receivable processes influence the relationships between companies. Efficient and accurate accounts payable practices ensure timely payments to suppliers, fostering strong vendor relationships and potential negotiating favorable terms. Similarly, effective accounts receivable practices, such as prompt and accurate invoicing and payment collection, enhance customer satisfaction and strengthen customer relationships.

The accounts payable and accounts receivable processes are interconnected and flow between companies. The accounts payable process involves managing payments owed to suppliers, while the accounts receivable process deals with payments owed by customers. These processes connect through purchase orders, sales orders, invoicing, recording in accounting systems, payment processing, cash flow impact, reconciliation, reporting, and relationship management. Understanding this connection and flow is essential for maintaining financial stability, managing vendor and customer relationships, and ensuring the smooth functioning of business transactions.

Training Employees for Accounts Payables and Receivables Functions

Training individuals to perform accounts payable and accounts receivable functions effectively is crucial for maintaining accurate financial records, managing cash flow, and ensuring smooth business operations. Here is a comprehensive guide on how to train people to perform these functions:

1. **Understand the Roles and Responsibilities:** Before initiating the training process, it is essential to clearly define the roles and responsibilities of accounts payable and accounts receivable personnel. Accounts payable professionals are responsible for managing supplier invoices, processing payments, and maintaining vendor relationships. Accounts receivable personnel handle customer invoicing, payment collection, and maintaining customer relationships. Understanding these roles helps tailor the training program to specific job requirements.

2. **Develop a Training Plan:** Create a structured training plan that outlines the objectives, topics, and timeline for each training session. Identify the key areas to cover, such as invoice processing, payment handling, vendor/customer management, record-keeping, and software/system proficiency. Break down the training into modules or sessions based on the complexity and level of expertise required.

3. **Provide an Overview of Accounting Principles:** To ensure a strong foundation, introduce the trainees to basic accounting principles relevant to accounts payable and accounts receivable. Cover concepts like double-entry bookkeeping, accrual accounting, revenue recognition, and expense matching. Explain how these principles impact the day-to-day tasks and financial reporting.

4. **Familiarize Trainees with Relevant Tools and Systems:** Accounts payable and accounts receivable professionals work with various tools and software systems. Trainees should become proficient in using accounting software, spreadsheets, and any other relevant applications. Provide hands-on training on data entry, generating reports, reconciling accounts, and performing routine tasks using the tools they will be working with.

5. **Invoice Processing and Management:** In the accounts payable training, focus on teaching trainees how to process supplier invoices accurately. Cover topics like verifying invoice details, matching invoices with purchase orders and receipts, coding invoices, and obtaining necessary approvals. Trainees should learn about common invoice discrepancies, exception handling, and resolution processes.

6. **Payment Handling and Cash Management:** Accounts payable training should include payment processing and cash management. Trainees should

understand different payment methods, such as checks, electronic funds transfers, and online payment systems. Teach them how to manage payment terms, handle payment discrepancies, and maintain proper documentation for audit purposes.

7. **Vendor/Customer Management:** Accounts payable and accounts receivable professionals interact with vendors and customers regularly. Trainees should learn effective communication and relationship management skills. Cover topics such as vendor/customer onboarding, resolving inquiries, handling disputes, and building collaborative partnerships. Emphasize the importance of professionalism, responsiveness, and maintaining positive business relationships.

8. **Record-Keeping and Documentation:** Accurate record-keeping is critical in both accounts payable and accounts receivable functions. Trainees should learn how to organize and maintain records, including invoices, receipts, payment confirmations, and other relevant documents. Teach them about compliance requirements, retention policies, and data security practices.

9. **Reporting and Analysis:** Accounts payable and accounts receivable professionals often generate reports and perform data analysis. Trainees should be familiarized with report generation, financial analysis, and key performance indicators relevant to their roles. Teach them how to interpret reports,

identify trends, and use the data to make informed decisions.

10. **Workflow and Process Optimization:** Efficiency and process optimization are essential for effective accounts payable and accounts receivable functions. Trainees should be encouraged to identify bottlenecks, suggest improvements, and streamline workflows. Introduce concepts like automation, digitization, and best practices for enhancing efficiency and reducing errors.

11. **Continuous Learning and Professional Development:** Encourage trainees to pursue continuous learning and professional development in the field of accounts payable and accounts receivable. This can include attending relevant workshops, seminars, webinars, or obtaining professional certifications. Foster a culture of growth and encourage trainees to stay updated with industry trends and regulations.

12. **Hands-on Practice and Feedback:** Throughout the training program, provide ample opportunities for trainees to practice what they have learned. Offer hands-on exercises, case studies, and real-world scenarios to simulate the actual work environment. Provide constructive feedback and guidance to help them improve their skills and confidence.

13. **Ongoing Support and Mentoring:** Even after the initial training, it is important to provide ongoing support and mentoring to the accounts payable and

accounts receivable personnel. Assign experienced mentors or supervisors who can guide and assist them in their day-to-day tasks. Conduct periodic reviews, address any challenges, and provide additional training as needed.

By following these steps, organizations can effectively train individuals to perform accounts payable and accounts receivable functions with confidence, accuracy, and efficiency. Well-trained personnel contribute to better financial management, improved cash flow, and stronger relationships with vendors and customers.

CHAPTER FIFTEEN
The Aging Report

An aging report is a financial document that provides a snapshot of a company's accounts receivable and their aging status. It categorizes outstanding receivable balances based on the length of time the invoices have been outstanding. The report is typically organized into different time periods, such as 0-30 days, 31-60 days, 61-90 days, and over 90 days.

The aging report works by examining the open invoices and determining how long each has been outstanding. It provides a breakdown of the total amount owed by customers in each time period. This information helps identify potential collection issues and allows the company to take appropriate actions to improve cash flow.

The aging report is important for several reasons:

1. **Cash Flow Management:** The report provides insights into the aging of receivables, allowing the company to assess the impact on cash flow. It helps identify which customers are slow to pay and highlights overdue accounts. By monitoring the aging report, companies can better anticipate cash inflows and manage working capital.

2. **Collection Prioritization:** The report helps prioritize collection efforts by focusing on overdue accounts. It allows the company to allocate resources effectively, concentrating on customers with the highest outstanding balances or those with the

longest payment delays. By identifying and addressing collection issues promptly, the company can improve its chances of receiving timely payments.

3. **Creditworthiness Assessment:** The aging report aids in evaluating the creditworthiness of customers. It provides a historical record of payment patterns and identifies customers who consistently pay late or have a higher risk of defaulting. This information is useful for setting credit limits, renegotiating terms, or determining whether to extend credit to new customers.

4. **Financial Reporting:** The aging report is essential for accurate financial reporting. It assists in estimating the allowance for doubtful accounts, which is a reserve set aside for potential bad debts. By analyzing the aging of receivables, the company can determine the appropriate amount to reserve, ensuring that financial statements reflect the true value of accounts receivable.

To improve aging report items, companies can implement the following strategies:

1. **Timely Invoicing:** Ensure that invoices are generated and sent to customers promptly. Delayed or incorrect invoices can lead to payment delays and negatively impact the aging report. Implement efficient invoicing processes and consider using automated systems to streamline the process.

2. **Clear Payment Terms:** Clearly communicate payment terms and expectations to customers. Ensure that the terms are stated on invoices and that customers are aware of the due dates. Regularly review and update payment terms as necessary.

3. **Collection Follow-up:** Implement a proactive approach to collections. Regularly monitor the aging report and establish a systematic follow-up process for overdue accounts. Contact customers promptly to remind them of outstanding balances and inquire about payment status. Maintain regular communication to address any concerns or issues that may be hindering timely payment.

4. **Customer Credit Assessment:** Conduct thorough credit assessments before extending credit to new customers. Review credit history, financial statements, and credit references to gauge their ability to pay. Establish appropriate credit limits based on the assessment.

5. **Payment Incentives and Penalties:** Consider offering incentives for early payment, such as discounts or rewards. Conversely, impose penalties for late payments, such as late fees or interest charges. These measures can encourage customers to pay promptly and reduce the number of overdue accounts.

6. **Collection Policies and Procedures:** Develop clear and consistent collection policies and procedures. Ensure that employees are trained on these policies

and understand their roles in the collection process. Maintain accurate documentation of collection activities to track progress and facilitate effective communication with customers.

Regularly reviewing the aging report, addressing overdue accounts promptly, and implementing strategies to improve payment collections can significantly impact the overall health of a company's accounts receivable and cash flow. By monitoring and managing the aging report effectively, companies can enhance their financial stability, maintain healthy customer relationships, and improve their overall operational performance.

The Aging Report, also known as the Accounts Receivable Aging Report, is a valuable tool used by businesses to track and manage their outstanding customer payments. It provides a detailed snapshot of the company's accounts receivable, categorizing unpaid invoices by their age, allowing businesses to identify and address potential collection issues. In this article, we will delve deeper into the Aging Report, its significance, and how it aids in effective accounts receivable management.

The Aging Report also assists in identifying potential collection issues. Delinquent accounts highlighted in the report can be addressed promptly, allowing businesses to follow up with customers and initiate collection efforts. The report provides valuable information for communication with customers, enabling businesses to track the history of payment delays, address any disputes or issues, and establish suitable payment arrangements. By promptly addressing delinquent accounts, businesses can improve their chances of recovering outstanding balances and maintaining positive customer relationships.

Furthermore, the Aging Report aids in evaluating the effectiveness of credit policies. By analyzing the report, businesses can assess the average time it takes for customers to pay their invoices and identify customers who consistently pay late. This information helps businesses determine if credit terms need to be revised, credit limits should be adjusted, or additional credit checks should be conducted before extending credit to new customers. By making informed decisions about credit policies, businesses can mitigate the risk of late payments and potential bad debt.

The Aging Report is also an essential tool for financial reporting and forecasting. It provides a clear picture of the company's accounts receivable position at a specific point in time, allowing businesses to assess their overall financial health. The report enables businesses to calculate the Days Sales Outstanding (DSO), which measures the average number of days it takes to collect payment from customers. DSO is a crucial metric for evaluating cash flow performance and comparing it against industry benchmarks. Additionally, the Aging Report provides valuable information for financial forecasting, allowing businesses to estimate future cash inflows and plan accordingly.

To generate an accurate Aging Report, businesses need to ensure that their accounts receivable records are up to date and accurate. This requires proper recording and tracking of customer payments and adjustments, timely application of payments to the corresponding invoices, and regular reconciliation of accounts receivable balances with the general ledger. Consistency and accuracy in maintaining accounts receivable records are essential for producing reliable Aging Reports.

The Benefits of the Aging Report

The Aging Report is a powerful tool for businesses to monitor and manage their accounts receivable. It provides a comprehensive overview of unpaid invoices categorized by their age, enabling businesses to track outstanding balances, identify delinquent accounts, and prioritize collection efforts. By analyzing the report, businesses can improve cash flow, identify potential collection issues, evaluate credit policies, and make informed decisions about customer relationships. The Aging Report plays a vital role in financial reporting, forecasting, and overall accounts receivable management, helping businesses maintain healthy cash flow and financial stability. The benefits of the aging reports are:

1. **Improved Cash Flow Management:**

   The Aging Report helps businesses monitor and manage their cash flow effectively. By categorizing outstanding invoices based on their age, businesses can identify which customers have overdue payments and take appropriate actions to collect those funds. By promptly addressing delinquent accounts, following up with customers, and initiating collection efforts, businesses can improve their cash flow, ensuring a steady inflow of funds to meet financial obligations and sustain operations.

2. Timely Identification of Potential Collection Issues:

The Aging Report enables businesses to identify potential collection issues at an early stage. By reviewing the report, businesses can identify customers with consistently overdue payments or those who frequently fall into the older age categories. This allows businesses to take proactive measures to address these issues, such as contacting customers for payment reminders, renegotiating payment terms, or initiating collection procedures. Early identification and resolution of collection issues can significantly reduce the risk of bad debt and improve the overall financial health of the business.

3. Accurate Financial Reporting and Analysis:

The Aging Report provides valuable information for financial reporting and analysis. It allows businesses to assess the overall health of their accounts receivable, track outstanding balances, and evaluate the effectiveness of credit policies. The report helps in calculating important financial metrics such as Days Sales Outstanding (DSO), which measures the average number of days it takes to collect payment from customers. These metrics provide insights into cash flow performance, customer payment trends, and potential areas for improvement. Accurate financial reporting and analysis based on the Aging Report help businesses make informed decisions and set realistic financial goals.

4. Improved Customer Relationship Management:

The Aging Report plays a significant role in managing customer relationships. By identifying delinquent accounts through the report, businesses can proactively communicate with customers regarding their outstanding balances. This communication helps address any payment disputes, resolve issues, and establish suitable payment arrangements. Taking prompt action based on the Aging Report demonstrates the business's commitment to maintaining positive customer relationships and ensures that concerns are addressed in a timely and professional manner. Effective customer relationship management leads to improved customer satisfaction and loyalty.

5. Evaluation and Improvement of Credit Policies:

The Aging Report serves as a valuable tool for evaluating the effectiveness of credit policies. By analyzing the report, businesses can assess the average time it takes for customers to pay their invoices and identify customers who consistently pay late. This information helps businesses determine if credit terms need to be revised, credit limits should be adjusted, or additional credit checks should be conducted before extending credit to new customers. Evaluating and adjusting credit policies based on the Aging Report helps mitigate the risk of late payments and potential bad debt, leading to a healthier accounts receivable portfolio.

The Aging Report holds great significance for businesses by providing a comprehensive overview of outstanding invoices categorized by their age. It facilitates improved cash flow management, timely identification of potential collection issues, accurate financial reporting and analysis, enhanced customer relationship management, evaluation and improvement of credit policies, enhanced financial forecasting and planning, and compliance and auditing purposes. By leveraging the benefits of the Aging Report, businesses can effectively manage their accounts receivable, improve financial performance, and foster long-term success.

CHAPTER SIXTEEN
The Most Popular Accounting Software

Accounting software plays a crucial role in modern business operations by automating financial processes, improving accuracy, and providing valuable insights into the financial health of a company. There are several accounting software options available, each with its own features and benefits. In this book, we will explore some popular accounting software solutions, discuss their key features, and highlight why they are important for businesses.

1. **QuickBooks:** QuickBooks is one of the most widely used accounting software packages for small and medium-sized businesses. It offers a range of features, including invoicing, expense tracking, bank reconciliation, financial reporting, and inventory management. QuickBooks also integrates with various third-party applications, making it a versatile tool for business management. Its user-friendly interface and robust functionality make it a popular choice for many businesses.

2. **Xero:** Xero is another popular cloud-based accounting software that caters to small businesses. It provides features such as invoicing, bank reconciliation, expense tracking, inventory management, and payroll processing. Xero also offers a user-friendly interface and supports integrations with various business applications, allowing for seamless data sharing. Additionally, it offers real-time collaboration, making it convenient

for business owners and their accountants to work together on financial matters.

3. **Sage Intacct:** Sage Intacct is a robust accounting software designed for small and midsize businesses. It offers features like general ledger, accounts payable and receivable, cash management, inventory management, and financial reporting. Sage Intacct provides advanced financial management capabilities and is highly scalable, making it suitable for growing businesses. It also offers integrations with other business applications, allowing for streamlined data flow across different systems.

4. **NetSuite:** NetSuite is a comprehensive cloud-based enterprise resource planning (ERP) system that includes accounting functionality. It provides features such as financial management, revenue recognition, order management, inventory management, and financial reporting. NetSuite offers a unified platform for managing various aspects of a business, making it ideal for medium-sized and large organizations. Its robust reporting and analytics capabilities help businesses gain valuable insights into their financial performance.

5. **FreshBooks:** FreshBooks is a cloud-based accounting software designed specifically for small businesses and self-employed professionals. It offers features like invoicing, expense tracking, time tracking, project management, and reporting. FreshBooks provides a simple and intuitive interface, making it easy for non-accounting professionals to

use. It also offers integrations with popular business tools, allowing for streamlined workflows.

6. **Wave:** Wave is a free accounting software aimed at small businesses and freelancers. It offers features like invoicing, expense tracking, bank reconciliation, and financial reporting. Wave is known for its user-friendly interface and simplicity. It provides basic accounting functionality at no cost, making it an attractive option for small businesses with limited budgets.

The choice of the best accounting software depends on several factors, including the size and nature of the business, specific accounting needs, budget constraints, and user preferences. What works for one business may not work for another. However, there are some common reasons why accounting software is important for businesses:

1. **Automation and Efficiency:** Accounting software automates manual financial tasks, such as data entry, calculations, and report generation. This saves time and improves efficiency, allowing businesses to focus on core activities. Automated processes also reduce the risk of human errors, ensuring greater accuracy in financial data.

2. **Financial Visibility and Reporting:** Accounting software provides real-time access to financial information, allowing businesses to monitor their financial health. It generates detailed financial reports, such as balance sheets, income statements, and cash flow statements, which provide insights

into profitability, liquidity, and overall performance. These reports help in making informed business decisions.

3. **Streamlined Financial Operations:** Accounting software streamlines various financial operations, including invoicing, payment processing, expense tracking, and bank reconciliation. It centralizes financial data, making it easily accessible and reducing the need for manual record-keeping. This simplifies financial management and improves overall control over financial processes.

4. **Compliance and Auditing:** Accounting software helps businesses maintain compliance with tax regulations and accounting standards. It automates tax calculations, generates tax forms, and ensures accurate financial records. Additionally, it facilitates the preparation of financial statements for external audits, simplifying the auditing process.

5. **Collaboration and Data Integration:** Many accounting software solutions offer collaboration features that allow business owners, accountants, and other stakeholders to work together on financial matters. They also integrate with other business applications, such as CRM systems and payroll software, enabling seamless data sharing and reducing duplicate data entry.

6. **Scalability and Growth:** As businesses grow, their accounting needs become more complex. Accounting software provides scalability, allowing

businesses to handle increasing volumes of financial transactions and data. It can accommodate multiple users, support multi-currency transactions, and provide advanced reporting and analysis capabilities, supporting business expansion.

To improve the aging report items, businesses can implement several strategies:

1. **Timely Invoicing and Payment Collection:** Ensure invoices are sent promptly and follow up on overdue payments. Offer incentives for early payment and establish clear credit terms. Regularly review the accounts receivable aging report to identify delinquent accounts and take appropriate actions.

2. **Effective Credit Management:** Evaluate the creditworthiness of customers before extending credit. Set appropriate credit limits based on the customer's financial stability and payment history. Monitor customer payment patterns and proactively address any issues or delays.

3. **Clear Communication:** Maintain open lines of communication with customers regarding outstanding balances and payment expectations. Send reminder notices, make courtesy calls, and establish a process for resolving disputes or discrepancies promptly.

4. **Streamlined Collection Processes:** Implement efficient collection procedures to escalate collection efforts when necessary. This may include sending

demand letters, engaging collection agencies, or pursuing legal action as a last resort. Regularly review collection strategies to optimize effectiveness.

5. **Regular Reconciliation:** Reconcile accounts receivable balances with customer statements regularly to identify any discrepancies. Promptly investigate and resolve any variances to ensure accurate reporting and prevent potential issues.

6. **Continuous Improvement:** Regularly review and analyze the aging report to identify trends and patterns. Look for opportunities to improve credit policies, streamline billing processes, or address common issues that lead to delayed payments. Implement changes based on insights gained from the aging report analysis.

By implementing these strategies, businesses can effectively manage their accounts receivable, reduce aging report items, improve cash flow, and strengthen customer relationships. Effective management of accounts receivable is crucial for maintaining a healthy financial position and ensuring the long-term success of a business.

CHAPTER SEVENTEEN
Myths About Financial Accounting

Financial accounting is a crucial aspect of running a business, providing essential information about a company's financial health, performance, and compliance. However, there are several myths and misconceptions surrounding financial accounting that can lead to misunderstandings and misinterpretations. In this article, we will debunk some common myths about financial accounting and shed light on the realities of this important discipline. While financial accounting is a well-established and widely understood field, there are some common myths or misconceptions that circulate among individuals. It's important to address these myths to ensure a clear understanding of the nature and purpose of financial accounting. Here are a few myths about financial accounting:

1. **Financial accounting is only about numbers:** One common myth is that financial accounting is purely a numbers game. In reality, financial accounting involves interpreting and communicating financial information to stakeholders, which requires analytical and interpretive skills. It goes beyond just crunching numbers to provide meaningful insights into a company's financial performance and position.

2. **Financial accounting is only for accountants:** Another myth is that financial accounting is solely the domain of accountants. While accountants play a crucial role in preparing and analyzing financial statements, financial accounting is relevant and

important for a wide range of professionals. Managers, investors, lenders, regulators, and other stakeholders rely on financial accounting information to make informed decisions.

3. **Financial accounting is rigid and inflexible:** Some believe that financial accounting follows strict rules and standards, leaving no room for interpretation or flexibility. While financial accounting adheres to generally accepted accounting principles (GAAP) or international financial reporting standards (IFRS), there is still judgment involved in applying these standards. Additionally, accounting standards are continually evolving to adapt to changing business practices and regulations.

4. **Financial accounting is only historical:** Another misconception is that financial accounting focuses solely on past events and historical data. While financial statements provide a historical perspective on a company's financial performance, they also serve as a basis for future decision-making. Financial accounting helps forecast future trends, assess risks, and make strategic business decisions based on historical financial data.

5. **Financial accounting is unnecessary due to technology:** With advancements in financial software and automation, some argue that financial accounting is becoming obsolete. However, technology complements rather than replaces financial accounting. While automation can streamline routine tasks, it still requires human

expertise to interpret financial data, exercise judgment, and ensure accuracy in financial reporting.

6. **Financial accounting is all about profit:** While profitability is an essential aspect of financial accounting, it is not the sole focus. Financial accounting encompasses a broader scope, including reporting on a company's assets, liabilities, equity, cash flows, and other financial metrics. It provides a comprehensive picture of a company's financial health, allowing stakeholders to assess its overall performance and sustainability.

7. **Financial Accounting is Only About Compliance:** Another misconception is that financial accounting is solely focused on regulatory compliance and meeting legal requirements. While compliance with accounting standards and regulations is indeed important, financial accounting serves a much broader purpose. It provides valuable information for decision-making, strategic planning, performance evaluation, and investor communication. Financial statements, such as the balance sheet, income statement, and cash flow statement, offer insights into a company's financial position, profitability, and cash flow, enabling stakeholders to assess the organization's overall performance.

8. **Financial Accounting is Only About Historical Data:** Some people believe that financial accounting is solely concerned with recording past financial transactions. While financial accounting does involve the recording and reporting of historical data,

it also plays a critical role in providing information for future decision-making. Financial statements and related analysis help in forecasting, budgeting, and setting financial goals. Historical financial data is used as a basis for projecting future trends and making informed predictions about a company's financial performance and viability.

9. **Financial Accounting is Inflexible and Rigid:** There is a misconception that financial accounting follows a fixed set of rules and is inflexible in adapting to changing business environments. While financial accounting adheres to generally accepted accounting principles (GAAP) or international financial reporting standards (IFRS), it is designed to accommodate various business structures and transactions. There is room for interpretation and judgment in applying accounting principles to specific circumstances. Additionally, accounting standards are periodically updated to reflect changes in business practices and address emerging issues, ensuring relevance and adaptability.

10. **Financial Accounting is Only for Large Companies:** Some believe that financial accounting is only relevant for large corporations with complex financial operations. However, financial accounting applies to businesses of all sizes, including small and medium-sized enterprises (SMEs) and even nonprofit organizations. Regardless of the scale of operations, financial accounting helps organizations maintain accurate records, assess financial performance, and fulfill their reporting obligations.

Financial statements provide crucial information for business owners, investors, lenders, and other stakeholders to evaluate the financial health and viability of an organization, irrespective of its size.

11. **Financial Accounting and Managerial Accounting:** Are the Same Financial accounting and managerial accounting are two distinct disciplines, often confused with one another. Financial accounting focuses on external reporting to stakeholders outside the organization, such as investors, creditors, and regulatory bodies. Managerial accounting, on the other hand, is geared towards providing internal information to aid in decision-making and operational management. While both disciplines involve the use of financial data, their objectives, scope, and audience differ significantly.

12. **Financial Accounting Can Predict Future Performance**: It is important to recognize that financial accounting is primarily concerned with reporting historical financial information rather than predicting future performance. While financial statements can provide insights into trends and indicators, they are not crystal balls that can accurately forecast future outcomes. Financial accounting provides a foundation for informed decision-making, but other factors, such as market dynamics, industry trends, and strategic initiatives, also influence future performance.

Debunking the myths about financial accounting is crucial to gaining a clear understanding of its purpose, relevance, and capabilities. Financial accounting is not limited to accountants or compliance alone; it encompasses the entire organization, provides insights for decision-making, incorporates historical and future-oriented perspectives, accommodates different business contexts, and serves organizations of all sizes. By dispelling these myths, businesses can embrace financial accounting as a valuable tool for assessing financial performance, facilitating informed decision-making, and driving sustainable growth.

It is important to dispel these myths to foster a clear understanding of financial accounting's role and significance. Financial accounting serves as the language of business, providing vital information for decision-making, accountability, and transparency. By debunking these myths, individuals can develop a more accurate appreciation for the field and its importance in the business world.

CHAPTER EIGHTEEN
Charts of Accounts

A chart of accounts is a systematic listing of all the individual accounts used by a business to record its financial transactions. It provides a structured framework for organizing and categorizing various types of accounts, enabling easy identification and tracking of financial information. The chart of accounts typically includes categories such as assets, liabilities, equity, revenues, and expenses.

Here are 10 examples of accounts that can be included in a chart of accounts:

1. **Cash:** This account represents the company's cash on hand or in bank accounts. It includes physical currency, checks, and electronic funds.

2. **Accounts Receivable:** This account records amounts owed to the company by customers for goods or services sold on credit.

3. **Inventory:** This account tracks the cost of the company's goods or products available for sale. It includes raw materials, work-in-progress, and finished goods.

4. **Accounts Payable:** This account represents the company's outstanding liabilities to vendors or suppliers for goods or services purchased on credit.

5. **Loans Payable:** This account records any long-term loans or borrowings that the company has incurred.

6. **Common Stock:** This account represents the equity invested by shareholders in the company.

7. **Sales Revenue:** This account records the income generated from the sale of goods or services.

8. **Cost of Goods Sold:** This account represents the direct costs associated with producing or acquiring the goods sold by the company.

9. **Salaries Expense:** This account tracks the wages or salaries paid to employees of the company.

10. **Rent Expense:** This account records the cost of renting or leasing premises for the business operations.

These examples demonstrate the range of accounts that can be included in a chart of accounts. However, it's important to note that the specific accounts included will vary depending on the nature of the business, its industry, and its unique financial requirements. The chart of accounts serves several purposes within the financial accounting system. Firstly, it provides a standardized framework for recording and categorizing financial transactions. By using a consistent set of accounts, it becomes easier to track and analyze financial information.

The chart of accounts facilitates the preparation of financial statements. The balances in each account are used to generate the balance sheet, income statement, and statement of cash flows. These statements provide important information about the financial health and performance of the business. Furthermore, the chart of accounts helps in budgeting and financial planning. By organizing accounts into relevant categories, it becomes easier to allocate funds, monitor expenses, and identify areas for cost control.

To illustrate how a chart of accounts works, let's consider an example transaction:

Suppose a company receives $1,000 in cash from a customer as payment for services provided. The journal entry to record this transaction would be:

Cash (Asset) $1,000 Service Revenue (Revenue) $1,000

In this entry, the cash account is debited with $1,000, representing an increase in cash. The service revenue account is credited with $1,000, reflecting the increase in revenue.

By using the chart of accounts, this transaction can be easily recorded and classified. The cash account would be assigned the account number for assets, and the service revenue account would be assigned the account number for revenues.

Chart of accounts is a fundamental tool in financial accounting. It provides a structured framework for organizing and classifying financial transactions. By using a chart of accounts, businesses can ensure accurate recording of transactions, facilitate financial reporting, and support effective financial management and decision-making.

The Purpose of Charts of Accounts

The chart of accounts is a key component of the financial accounting system for any organization. It serves the purpose of organizing and categorizing financial transactions into distinct accounts, enabling the company to track and report its financial activities accurately. The chart of accounts provides a structured framework that ensures consistency and facilitates the preparation of financial statements, analysis of financial data, and compliance with regulatory requirements.

The primary purposes of a chart of accounts are as follows:

1. **Organization and Classification:** The chart of accounts organizes financial transactions into categories, making it easier to classify and track specific types of accounts. It provides a systematic structure for grouping similar accounts together, such as assets, liabilities, equity, revenues, and expenses.

2. **Consistency and Standardization:** By implementing a chart of accounts, businesses can ensure consistency and standardization in their financial reporting. It establishes uniformity in the naming and numbering of accounts, allowing for easier understanding and interpretation of financial information.

3. **Financial Reporting:** The chart of accounts forms the basis for generating financial statements such as the balance sheet, income statement, and cash flow statement. Each account in the chart contributes to the accurate presentation of financial data in these reports, providing stakeholders with a clear understanding of the company's financial position and performance.

4. **Analysis and Decision-Making:** An appropriately structured chart of accounts facilitates financial analysis by providing a logical framework for examining different aspects of the business. It enables stakeholders to analyze revenue and expense trends, track key performance indicators, and make informed decisions based on reliable financial data.

5. **Regulatory Compliance:** Many regulatory bodies and tax authorities require companies to follow specific reporting standards and guidelines. A well-designed chart of accounts ensures compliance with these requirements, making it easier to provide accurate financial information for tax purposes and regulatory reporting.

Setting up a Chart of Accounts for a Company:

1. **Understand the Business:** Gain a thorough understanding of the company's operations, industry, and unique financial requirements. This understanding will help determine the specific accounts needed in the chart of accounts.

2. **Determine Account Categories:** Identify the main categories of accounts required for financial reporting, such as assets, liabilities, equity, revenues, and expenses. Each category will have subcategories or individual accounts that capture specific financial transactions.

3. **Design Account Numbering System:** Develop a logical numbering system for accounts within each category. The numbering system should be intuitive and consistent, making it easy to identify the purpose and classification of each account.

4. **Account Naming:** Establish clear and descriptive names for each account that accurately represent its purpose. The names should be concise, yet provide enough information to distinguish one account from another.

5. **Customize the Chart:** Tailor the chart of accounts to the specific needs of the company. This may involve adding or removing accounts, creating subcategories, or modifying the default structure to align with the company's unique reporting requirements.

6. **Consider Future Growth:** Anticipate the company's future needs and expansion plans when designing the chart of accounts. Ensure it can accommodate new accounts or changes in business operations without major disruptions or reorganization.

7. **Review and Validation:** Before finalizing the chart of accounts, seek input and feedback from stakeholders such as accountants, financial analysts, and senior management. Validate the structure and account definitions to ensure accuracy and alignment with the company's goals and objectives.

8. **Documentation and Communication:** Document the finalized chart of accounts, including the account names, numbers, and descriptions. Communicate the chart to relevant personnel, including accounting staff, to ensure consistent and accurate use of accounts in financial transactions.

It's important to note that the chart of accounts may evolve over time as the company's operations change or new reporting requirements emerge. Regular reviews and updates are necessary to maintain its relevance and effectiveness. The chart of accounts serves a vital role in organizing, classifying, and tracking financial transactions within a company. It provides a structured framework that enhances consistency, accuracy, and efficiency in financial reporting. By carefully designing and setting up the chart of accounts, businesses can streamline their accounting processes, gain valuable insights from financial data, and meet regulatory compliance requirements.

Benefits of Charts of Accounts

The chart of accounts is typically divided into different categories and levels to facilitate efficient financial reporting and analysis. The categories can include assets, liabilities, equity, revenue, and expenses. Each account within these categories is assigned a unique code or number, allowing for easy identification and classification.

The primary purpose of a chart of accounts is to establish consistency and uniformity in financial reporting. By providing a standardized structure, it ensures that financial transactions are recorded consistently across all departments and business units. This uniformity enables accurate comparison of financial data over time and across different entities within an organization.

Here are some key benefits of a chart of accounts:

1. **Organizational Structure:** The COA can be tailored to reflect the organizational structure of the business. It allows for the segregation of financial information by departments, locations, projects, or any other relevant categorization. This hierarchical arrangement helps in the analysis of financial performance at various levels of the organization.

2. **Reporting and Analysis:** A well-designed chart of accounts simplifies financial reporting and analysis. It provides a framework for generating various financial statements, such as the balance sheet, income statement, and cash flow statement. With the accounts appropriately classified and grouped, stakeholders can easily identify and extract the relevant information for decision-making and performance evaluation.

3. **Compliance and Regulations:** The COA plays a vital role in ensuring compliance with accounting standards and regulations. By aligning the chart of accounts with relevant financial reporting requirements, businesses can accurately report their financial information and meet the necessary compliance obligations. This is particularly important for publicly traded companies that need to adhere to strict reporting guidelines.

4. **Cost Tracking and Budgeting:** A well-structured COA allows for effective tracking of costs and expenses. By assigning specific accounts to different cost centers, projects, or activities, businesses can accurately monitor and control their expenditures. The COA also facilitates budgeting and variance analysis, enabling comparisons between planned and actual financial performance.

5. **Scalability and Flexibility:** As businesses grow and evolve, their financial reporting needs may change. The chart of accounts can accommodate such changes and provide the flexibility to add new accounts or modify existing ones. This scalability allows organizations to adapt their financial reporting system to meet their evolving requirements without disrupting their overall reporting structure.

6. **Integration with Accounting Systems:** The COA serves as the backbone for accounting software systems. It provides a standardized framework for integrating financial transactions, ensuring accurate and efficient data processing. Accounting software

often comes with predefined COA templates that can be customized to fit the specific needs of the business.

7. **Facilitation of Audits and Due Diligence:** A well-maintained chart of accounts simplifies audits and due diligence processes. It provides a clear and organized structure for auditors to analyze financial records, verify transactions, and assess the overall financial health of the organization. A well-structured COA can expedite audit procedures and enhance transparency during due diligence exercises.

A chart of accounts is a fundamental component of the financial accounting system. It provides a structured framework for organizing financial information, ensuring consistency in reporting, facilitating analysis and decision-making, enabling compliance with regulations, and supporting efficient financial management. A well-designed and maintained chart of accounts is essential for businesses to effectively track and report their financial transactions, ultimately leading to informed decision-making and sound financial management.

About the Author

Dr. Lester Reid is a professional with a diverse background in accounting, finance, taxation, data analytics, business management, research, and publication. With extensive experience and expertise in multiple fields, he has established himself as a transformational leader, speaker, and consultant. He is a professional accountant, tax practitioner and financial management expert.

Dr. Reid earned his Doctor of Business in Management from Grand Canyon University, where he focused on the areas of business management. He holds several master's degrees, including a Master of Taxation from Mississippi State University, a Master of Accounting, a Master of Science in Management, a Master of Business Administration from Texas A&M University, and a Master of Education in Adult and Higher Education from University of Houston. His educational journey began with a Bachelor of Business Administration in Accounting and a Bachelor of Business Administration in Finance from Florida Atlantic University. He also holds an Associate of Arts in Business Management from Palm Beach State College.

Driven by a passion for learning and professional development, Dr. Reid is currently pursuing his Doctor of Business Administration in Accounting at West Virginia University. He is committed to expanding his knowledge and skills to stay at the forefront of his field.

Dr. Reid's expertise extends beyond academia. He has earned professional designations and certifications, including Six Sigma certifications at various levels, such as Six Sigma: Black Belt, Green Belt, Yellow Belt, and White Belt. These certifications reflect his proficiency in process improvement and quality management methodologies. Additionally, he is Quality Matters certified, further demonstrating his commitment to maintaining high standards in education and training.

With a strong academic foundation and practical experience, Dr. Reid has served as a doctoral dissertation supervisor, subject matter expert, and content matter expert. He has guided aspiring scholars in their research endeavors, provided insights into complex subjects, and contributed to the advancement of knowledge in his areas of expertise.

As a transformational leader and speaker, Dr. Reid possesses excellent communication and motivational skills. He has the ability to inspire and empower individuals and teams to achieve their full potential. His extensive background in business and financial management allows him to provide valuable insights and guidance to organizations seeking strategic direction and growth.

Dr. Reid's professional career also includes consulting engagements, where he has leveraged his expertise to assist businesses in optimizing their financial and operational performance. His knowledge in accounting, finance, data analytics, and business management enables him to identify opportunities for improvement, implement effective strategies, and drive positive change within organizations.

Dr. Lester Reid is a respected professional in the fields of accounting, finance, taxation, data analytics, business management, and education. With a strong academic background, diverse range of degrees, professional certifications, and practical experience, he has become a sought-after expert, mentor, and consultant. Driven by a passion for continuous learning and professional growth, he continues to make significant contributions to his fields of expertise.

Dr. Lester Reid

www.ingramcontent.com/pod-product-compliance
Lightning Source LLC
Chambersburg PA
CBHW060332200326
41519CB00011BA/1914